DOMIN

THE PERFECT PUPPY PROJECT

The ultimate no-mess, zero-stress, step-by-step guide to raising the perfect puppy

Published by

Elite Publishing Academy
www.ElitePublishingAcademy.com

First Edition published 2019
© Dominic Hodgson 2019

Printed and bound in Great Britain
www.ElitePublishingAcademy.com

A catalogue record for this book is available from The British Li-
brary

ISBN 978-1-912713-14-1

To my own two pups, Alex and Toby.

X

Contents

Praise for *The Perfect Puppy Project*

What dog trainers are saying about
The Perfect Puppy Project

"The Perfect Puppy book really highlights the journey for new puppy owners in a step by step and easy to follow plan. It guides you past the array of outdated information that is already out there, instead showing you how to raise them effectively and highlighting the importance of working kindly, patiently and consistently. This is something that gets missed but is the key ingredient for puppy training success.

The advice from Dom is fantastic, and should be at the top of every new puppy owners book list, to ensure that you get things right from the start.

There are no complicated or confusing elements in this book and that is perfect for anyone with a new puppy. Life can be complicated enough with them!

This book will help you to get the happy, confident and well behaved puppy that you want and will make your lives together so much easier and much more fulfilled, as they mature into an adult."

Claire Lawrence
www.highpeakdogservices.co.uk

"Such down to earth advise it's practically a Jules Verne Journey to the Centre of the Earth! When there are so many puppy books out there it's hard to believe that yet another could be so refreshingly different, and much more helpful.

It's easy to read, doesn't beat around the bush and is perfect for the first time pup owner or, perhaps more importantly, for the owner whose last puppy owning experience was not so pleasant! Another triumph for common sense dog training.

Karen Boyce

www.beastlythoughts.co.uk

"Dom has got it spot on again with his latest book! It's a workable plan to make sure your puppy really is perfect! Straightforward, easy to read and no-nonsense this book is ideal for brand new puppy owners who want to get it right. I will be recommending this to all of my puppy owners!"

Nicola Davies BA(Hons.) MAPDT 01059 CAP1

www.contentedcaninestraining.com

"I have never owned my own puppy all the dogs I have had myself I've adopted from as young as one year old. So having a puppy is totally new to me and this book is easy to read follow and understand. I love that it is written in Dominic's Straight Forward No Nonsense Style just like his 'How to be your dog's Superhero' Book which is my favourite. When I get my puppy I will have everything I need in place and ready to go so I have my very own Perfect Puppy!"

Suzanne Gould

www.edinburghholisticdogs.co.uk

"This is an excellent book for all owners, (or about to be owners), of a new puppy. It is written in easy to understand sections, guiding the new owner through all the stages and training that a puppy needs in its' first weeks and months with them. It carefully shows the new owner the best way to train their puppy so that it becomes a wonderful companion dog.

The accompanying free online resources are sure to be a great help to the new owner in fully understanding how to train their new puppy."
Fiona Henderson PPDTI Adv
Solihull Dog Training Club

"Hurrah! A real world training book that doesn't get bogged down with learning theory! There's no history of how dogs became dogs here – thank goodness. It does what it promises – a complete no BS guide to raising a perfect (or near perfect) puppy.

And that is just what we need, real world training for a real and often harsh world where dogs are frequently relinquished into an already overburdened rescue system or irresponsibly rehomed, passed around from pillar to post, behaviour problems worsening with each new owner until there is no hope left for that dog.

Through my background in rescue (where the #1 cause of dogs being abandoned is due to behaviour problems) I've seen thousands of new owners make the same mistakes time and time again. Who suffers? The dogs suffer. Enough is enough. Let's spread the key messages of this book far and wide.

The messages are simple. Dogs do what works. Dogs do what dogs enjoy and find rewarding. Play, Eat, Sleep, Repeat. Find your dog's Kryptonite. The methods are easy to follow and when he comes to dispelling the myths about socialization and training proper handling skills – Dom's techniques literally become lifesavers. The onus is always placed exactly where it should be: on us the owners. Puppy has done something you didn't want them to? Roll up a newspaper and hit yourself over the head with it. Dom's style is engaging and funny. He has created an accessible, readable little book aimed at those who need it most; first time puppy owners.

You may even discover the secret of what all dogs really want to know, that is, how to be a Good Boy. Go forth all ye First Time Puppy Owners into the world of happy, responsible lifelong dog ownership."
Katie Guastapaglia - Enrichment Specialist at Dogwood Adventure Play
www.dogwoodadventureplay.com

"The Perfect Puppy Recipe is the latest book from Best Selling Author and Dog Trainer Dom Hodgson. Dom has once again managed to explain the joys, pitfalls and solutions to raising a well behaved and adjusted puppy in easy to understand language.

His common sense approach and jargon free way of explaining the best way to raise your puppy makes a fresh change from the more traditional dog training book out there. If you are expecting a book full of complicated dog training jargon and stuffed full of learning theory then this is not the book for you. If, however, you are looking for a book that even the most inexperienced dog person will find easy to understand and enjoyable to read then this is the book for you.

The Perfect Puppy Recipe will take you by the hand and will guide you through the process of introducing your puppy to her new home, socialisation, toilet training and early training. It really is one book I will make sure all my new but especially first time puppy owners read."

Natasja Lewis DipCABT - Canine Development Coach and Behaviourist
www.nightsabredogtraining.co.uk

"A must read for first time puppy owners! No messing, no fluff, straight talking, fabulous advice to get it right the first time. This is the book to read if you want to avoid a little biting, barky, whinging, jumping up, and running off Tasmanian devil!

Cute as they may be, I see many owners who end up pulling their hair out at their pup's antics, causing an incredible amount of stress and heartache, hardly mans best friend. If only they could have read this book when puppy arrived they would have had a much more fun and enjoyable time and in turn a lifetime of making amazing memories with their pet.

This book will save you hundreds if not thousands of pounds and hours with a professional in future, for less than £20!

I see how it goes wrong all the time, even with the best intentions. This book has all the answers you need to avoid it!

Very easy to read, understand and put into practice with some great examples. This book really will set you up to have a fabulous dog. One I will certainly be recommending to clients and friends who have a puppy for the first time."
Sarah Bartlett
www.houndhelpers.co.uk

"Getting a puppy is a huge responsibility; you are responsible for shaping your new bundle of fluff into a well-balanced, happy hound. This book is the blue print for making sure you get off on the right foot. The no BS approach is simple to follow with a good dollop of humour thrown in too. A must read for any new puppy parent."

Tam Wilson
www.born2runpetcare.com

"What a great little book for owners bringing home a new puppy. Easy to read and understand and most importantly no jargon. It explains about implementing an excellent routine with a new puppy which many owners either don't know about, don't understand the importance of or just forget once they get that new, cute little puppy home.

The important thing now is getting this book to new puppy owners. Dom has again managed to write with humour which makes you want to keep reading. A very enjoyable read."

Bev Smith RGN, KCAI (CD)
www.inlinedogtraining.co.uk

The Perfect Puppy Project

Prologue

"So many things to see, people to do".
Neil Gaiman

The exact second you bring your new puppy home from the breeders, you are effectively turning over a giant egg timer with around eight weeks' worth of sand in it.

Obviously, owning a dog is a lifelong commitment, and your new four-legged friend is going to require a big investment of time, effort and commitment from you, for at least the next 10 years, hopefully a lot longer.

But the first six months is when you mould your puppy into the dog you want him to be, and the first three months are when the foundation stones are put in place.

This makes the first few days and weeks critical. And if you are a first-time puppy owner who has never done this before, then it's natural to feel shit-scared and overwhelmed with all the information being thrown at you from well-meaning friends and family.

That's because the first time we do anything new in life, it's usually pretty scary.

When I was five I learned to ride my first bike with my dad running along behind me, holding the seat steady to stop me from falling over, and whispering words of encouragement until I finally gathered enough speed for him to let go.

Could I have learned to ride a bike on my own? Probably, but it wouldn't have happened as quickly *or* been as enjoyable.

I had the pleasure of repeating this experience with my two boys when they first learned to ride their bikes.

We all need a helping hand now and again

Having a 'helping hand' to guide me through tough times has held me in good stead ever since.

When I started my first dog adventure business I was incredibly lucky to stumble upon some fantastic dog training *and* business mentors, whose no-nonsense approach has helped me achieve success much faster than I would have had I done it all on my own.

And that is the gift I want to give to you with this book.

The Perfect Puppy Project gives you a step-by-step, easy-to-follow plan to ensure you have a worry-free puppy experience.

Much like the other dog training books I've written, there is no flannel, fluff or fancy dog training talk for you to get your head around.

I promise everything in the next 10 chapters will be useful, interesting, easy to understand *and* fun to implement with your new puppy.

This means if you are a fluffy-bunny, science-speaking dog trainer who is looking for the next 'hot new thing' then you will be sorely disappointed. Please send the book back to me and I'll happily give you a refund. I don't want you reading it and I don't care what you think about the book either, so don't bother sending me feedback.

No. This book is for Mr and Mrs 'First-time puppy owner', who are bursting with excitement, and fizzing with fear about the thought of welcoming a new puppy into their home.

It's for those first-time pup parents who are desperate to get it right first time but are honest enough to admit they know 'sod-all' about raising, owning and caring for a puppy.

It's for the new dog owner who wants to know how to raise a puppy with the minimum stress possible, so they can enjoy a hassle-free life with their new dog.

Why you need this book

That sand is going to fall pretty quickly from one end of the egg timer to the other, and as it runs out, so does the window of opportunity you have to give your puppy the best start in life.

And as pleasurable as it is, you simply don't have time to sit indoors and cuddle your puppy 24/7.

Your new puppy really does have "so many things to see, people to do". And not just people either. Over the next 90 days you are about to lead your puppy on a guided tour through the museum of life.

How your future dog behaves at home, in the park, in restaurants, with friends, with strangers, with dogs, cats and everything else is all dependent upon the experience you provide for him in the next three to six months.

We have a *lot* to do.

I don't want you to be intimidated by the list of things you need to do over the next few months, but rather take it as a clear sign you need to get organised.

There's a world of activities and experiences out there for you and your dog to enjoy, but many of those can wait until your dog is more mature, obedient and ready to learn.

However, there are some experiences you NEED to ensure your puppy has immediately.

The Puppy 'Project'

Most of the books I've written to date include some kind of plan of action to get you quickly and easily implementing what you learn. I'm usually happy to let the reader consume and use whatever information they require at that particular time, much like visiting a buffet.

This book is *different*.

It's more of a set menu, and I'd like you to try each and every course.

I've laid out for you a clear day-by-day, week-by-week plan of action I suggest you follow closely.

I've called it a 'puppy project' for a reason. The Cambridge Dictionary defines a project as

a piece of *planned work* or an activity that is finished over a period of time and intended to achieve a *particular purpose*.

Well, this book provides a **plan** that guides you from the moment you pick your puppy up from the breeder's to around the time he is six months old.

And the **purpose** of this book is to do everything possible to turn your lovable puppy into an easy-to-manage and well-behaved dog that you are proud to take anywhere.

In many ways there's never been a better time to be a dog, or a dog owner. There's a never-ending array of products and services available to satisfy even the fussiest dog, or dog owner. The commercial Big Bang has brought an explosion of choice in the pet industry, and with it many new sources of information.

You may be an inexperienced dog owner, or perhaps it's been a while since you owned a dog, and so naturally you are desperate to get off on the right foot and make as few mistakes as possible.

So who can you trust to provide advice at this crucial time?

That's an interesting question.

Choose your doggy guru wisely

As a new puppy owner, you will be bombarded with advice from well-meaning but often clueless relatives and friends who own dogs, or have owned them in the past. Sadly, owning a dog no more qualifies you to be an expert in dog training than owning a car qualifies you to be a mechanic, or owning a vagina qualifies you to be a gynaecologist.

So we will take advice from friends and family with a pound of salt.

Then you've got crackpot dog astrologists and other 'spiritual' dog trainers, who will happily suggest incense remedies and healing crystals to align your canine chakras and fix your dog training problems. If that's your cup of chai then go ahead and trust your luck. But in my humble, honest and accurate opinion, these charlatans are unlikely and unable to give you any practical dog training advice to help you train your puppy. You'd be better off asking the cat for dog training advice …

And in this ever-connected world we live in, you don't even have to pay for advice. You can get easy access to hundreds of hours of dog training videos on YouTube, or ask questions in free Facebook groups. And you will be presented with many leaflets and brochures from insurance companies when you pick up your registered puppy, not to mention pet food manufacturers who all have their own agendas in mind, not necessarily yours …

There is some good advice to be found online, but in my experience the best dog trainers are out there enjoying their own dogs, or helping distressed dog owners fix theirs. It's the empty-vessel dog trainers, or (god forbid) the 'dog enthusiasts' who frequent the free message boards of the World Wide Web, spewing out their stupid opinions about dogs onto unsuspecting dog owners like you. Enter at your peril, but in most cases avoid these keyboard warriors like the plague.

And don't think just because someone has a professional qualification they are the best person to help you raise your puppy. All over the world there are dog trainers who permit and actively encourage dog-to-dog play in their 'puppy parties'. In far too many cases the puppies aren't playing at all, but rather they are learning to 'play-fight'. These unfortunate puppies progress from puppy parties to 'dog park raves', and become a nightmare for the owners to exercise.

I'll go into greater detail about why you should avoid puppy parties in chapter 8 but it's worth attending a local dog training class without your dog so you can suss out what kind of operation they are running. If they don't let you, then they obviously have something to hide.

Even your local vet may give some advice that if followed to the letter, can actually hinder your puppy's development. I'm talking about the insane instructions recommending you don't take your puppy outside until his vaccinations are complete.

Your puppy will probably get his first vaccination at eight weeks old, or as soon as you collect him from the breeder. Then he gets the second vaccination two weeks later, along with the instruction to keep him at home and only take him outside two weeks later.

Well, that can easily take you up to 14 weeks, and by then you only have two weeks left of the socialisation period, which sadly is not enough time for you to give your puppy the adequate socialisation experiences he requires.

There are many outstanding dog trainers working today, and I've been fortunate enough to learn from, and in many cases work alongside, the most knowledgeable and respected in the world.

Sadly, the voice of the sensible minority of trainers is being lost in the static noise emanating from namby-pamby 'dog trainers' who dominate the social media scene.

That's why I've written this book. *The Puppy Project* provides you with the common-sense, joined-up thinking you need to provide your puppy gets the safe home-schooling and sensible socialisation he needs.

And to help you more quickly settle in your new puppy, I've also included a stack of audio and video bonuses you can access straight away. These in-depth trainings will add some meat to the bones of what I teach in this book. To access your free bonuses go to:

www.mydogssuperhero.com/perfectpuppyproject

So without further ado, let's take a look at why welcoming a cute little bundle of fluff and bones into your home is so life changing and terrifying …

The Perfect Puppy Project

Introduction

"A life without a dog is a mistake".
Carl Zuckmayer

There's life BC, and there's life AD, but I'm in no way religious, and in this instance BC stands for Before Canine.

Before Canine

Life **B**efore **C**anine is distinctly easier than life AD.

Depending on your age you may have a job and a partner, maybe a mortgage, and if you are really unlucky children too. Just kidding, dear reader, as a father of two boys I can highly recommend having children. Although dogs are better, obviously.

The Perfect Puppy Project

Some people remain forever in the state of Before Canine, and through choice or circumstance never get to enjoy the pleasure of owning and sharing their life with a dog.

Weirdos.

But <u>you</u> are different.

You bought this book, so I'm guessing you have left or will soon be leaving BC in the past, and entering the next phase of your life. AD.

AKA life *After Dog.*

After Dog

To say life After Dog is somewhat different to life Before Canine would be the understatement of the century.

You have a new role in life, with new responsibilities to fulfil, and a reason to get up in the morning, whether you want to or not. You also have a perfect excuse not to attend those pain in the arse parties your friends invite you to. *"Sorry, we've got to get back for the dog …".* You can conveniently fail to mention your dog will be happily sleeping in his crate and won't care if you are 'out' for a few hours.

But without putting too fine a point on it, life after dog is different and can be bloody hard work.

For most dog owners, life AD is different *and* way more enjoyable than life BC.

The new puppy brings joy to the home, and a sense of love and friendship you just can't get from any other animal.

It profoundly changes your life, and once you've crossed the canine Rubicon and moved from BC to AD, you almost never go back and will remain hooked on hounds for life.

For many other dog owners though, life AD is different *and* challenging, and *not* in a good way.

The challenging canine

Some challenges in life are manageable and even enjoyable.

Running a half-marathon is an immensely rewarding challenge. I've done it so I know first-hand this is true.

I would imagine, and I'll have to imagine because I've never done it, that climbing Mount Everest is a more difficult challenge. I know without the proper training, equipment and guidance I would likely end up failing that challenge, and possibly even falling to the ground then disappearing into a puff of smoke, like Wile E Coyote in the Roadrunner cartoons.

The success you have overcoming any challenge comes down to how well prepared you are before you start, and how few mistakes you make along the way.

This book prepares you fully for the challenge of raising a puppy. It contains enough knowledge to prevent you from making the crucial mistakes that could mean you end up hating your puppy-raising experience and wishing you'd got a cat instead.

The Perfect Puppy Project

Are you ready for a dog?

I've met many dog owners who genuinely feel their life was a LOT easier before they got a dog. They confess the stress far outweighs the pleasure they get from owning one. Please understand, these aren't bad people, but at some point along the puppy path, they made some bad choices which ended up ruining their puppy, and with it their chances of the puppy developing into a trusted member of the family.

I know this to be true because I made many of the same mistakes with my first puppy too, and I shall be coming clean on all of 'Dom's Big Fat Puppy Cock-ups' during the book.

There are many reasons why some dog owners don't enjoy the experience, and eventually they feel the situation has become so irrevocable they give their dog up.

Maybe they shouldn't have got a dog in the first place?

Despite what you might think, dog ownership *isn't* for everyone. And much like a pineapple-topped pizza, you won't know if you like being a dog owner until you've tried it.

However, unlike the pineapple-topped pizza, an unwanted dog isn't quite as easy to discard.

Or at least it shouldn't be.

The number of dogs who are put up for rescue at eight months old (i.e. the age they start transforming from cute puppy to delinquent teenage tearaway dogs) would suggest otherwise.

You wouldn't think it possible our throwaway society would extend to dogs, but heart-breakingly, it happens every day. It doesn't matter what the breed of the dog or what class of society the dog owner comes from. Potentially perfect puppies who weren't given the right guidance develop into difficult dogs and get moved on to rescue centres, all the time.

Why I love non-dog-owning dog lovers

I meet loads of responsible non-dog-owners all the time. These are people who say, *"I would love to have a dog but I just don't have the time to look after one."*

Yes! I think to myself. This person gets it. They know how stressful, demanding and time intensive owning a dog can be, and they also know their current life situation isn't compatible with owning a dog. So they don't get one.

Responsible non-dog-owners, I salute you!

The much more common path, which leads inevitably to problems, is when someone acquires a puppy and then realises a short while later that they don't have enough time to devote to the dog.

What is it really like to own a dog?

You would think, even if you haven't owned a dog before, that you could easily guess what life AD will be like …

For example, it costs money to own a dog, and big dogs eat more than small dogs, so they cost more too. No shit, Sherlock.

Yes, and big dogs have bigger shits than small dogs, although it all fits in a poo bag, so you don't really have to worry about that.

Dogs are messy. Fact. And bearded or slobbery breeds are generally messier than those who have clean pointy faces.

Hairy dogs tend to shed their fur, so don't surprised if you are pulling hairs from your tongue every time you have a brew. It's all delicious and nutritious, honest.

There are some particularly useless dog owners who find it acceptable to get rid of a dog just so they can try another breed. But I'm guessing those idiots won't be reading this book. If that sounds like you, then give yourself a shake and sort your life out. You're a disgrace.

Quite often, the reason the relationship between owner and puppy breaks down is because the dog owner got the wrong kind of dog.

What's the right kind of puppy for you?

Everyone who wants and can afford a dog should be allowed to own one, but not every breed of dog is suitable for every owner.

When choosing a puppy it's easy to be seduced and swayed by attractive pictures of beautiful-looking gun dogs. But many pedigree dogs come with breed needs far beyond the capabilities of the average owner. And for the record, I consider myself an average dog owner. I work, I travel, I have kids and commitments which mean I can't be with my dogs 24/7. This means some breeds would be too much trouble and hassle for me to care for. So don't feel bad about passing over your first choice in favour of a breed more suited to your lifestyle.

Sometimes this mis-match is too difficult to overcome, and so getting the 'wrong dog' is another contributor to the overpopulation of rescue centres around the world.

Scum-of-the-earth puppy farmers also have a lot to answer for. Breeding puppies purely for profit is, in my eyes, totally abominable. Avoiding getting scammed with a farm-bred or backyard puppy should be your number-one priority. Often these poor dogs have suffered such physical and mental trauma at an early age that it's almost impossible to turn them into happy dogs you can live with, and it's certainly beyond the capabilities of most owners.

How to choose the perfect puppy for you

In this book I'm taking up the training story from the moment you bring your puppy home, but if you are at the stage of still looking for a puppy, then you should first think about the type of breed you want, which should be guided by how much time you want to spend training and exercising him.

Then in your quest to find the right puppy you should be more concerned about finding a genuine dog-loving breeder, rather than quibbling about whether to get a chocolate, apricot or red version of the breed you are looking for.

All of the above are valid reasons for giving up a dog, but they still represent the tip of the iceberg, and the main reason why dogs end up in rescue centres is simply because the owners can't control them.

The Perfect Puppy Project

Whodathunkit?

It's sad, but true.

The owners can't control the dog at home, and so they become destructive, which causes the owner to want to end the relationship and get rid of the dog.

Or they can't control the dog outside on *or* off lead, which makes for stressful, frustrating and sometimes painful walks. Yes, painful. Having your arm pulled out of its socket every time your dog lunges forward really hurts.

And just as painful to your pride is when you are constantly apologising to other dog owners because your dog has once again done something to embarrass you, all because <u>you didn't have enough control.</u> All this becomes too much for the dog owner to handle, and so the poor dog is given up.

The really sad thing is that, in most cases, this is completely avoidable.

With the right intentions and a plan of action, it's possible for almost every new owner to successfully raise a puppy who is relatively easy to look after, and even a pleasure to own.

Yes, getting a puppy is life changing in every sense, but you get to decide whether it's a life-enhancing or a life-diminishing event.

You hold the key to the future life with your dog.

How to use this book

I've written this book to be a complete no-BS guide to raising a perfect (or near perfect) puppy.

You'll find little in this book about the history of dogs, or what happens to the puppy while he's growing in his mummy's tummy, and nothing at all about how the daddy dog put him in there in the first place, phew!

This book provides a blueprint to show you exactly what to do at key moments in your puppy's development, and just as importantly, what you most definitely *shouldn't* do, from the moment you pick up your puppy until he is around six months old.

In my experience, if you get the first six months correct then you can generally enjoy a lifetime of stress-free fun with your family dog.

As with all my books, there's no flimflam or complicated dog trainer jargon. I'm going to share with you exactly what I think you should do if you want your puppy to be easy to look after and a pleasure to exercise.

Some of my views you will no doubt disagree with and find challenging. Not because they are in any way aversive, and will harm your puppy, but more because they will require you to inhabit a place I like to call 'the real world'.

See, in the real world not all dogs are easy to look after, which as we have seen leads to thousands of dogs given up every year. This is almost never the dog's fault, and instead it's because of something the owner unwittingly or unintentionally allowed to happen.

A Dogs Trust report in 2016 found the most common reason dogs are given up is because they have one or more problems the owners find difficult to live with.

These include dogs that:

- can't be left home alone because they are noisy or destructive, also known as separation anxiety.
- show signs of fear when they hear loud noises.
- show some signs of aggression (e.g. barking, lunging or growling) at other dogs when out for a walk.

All of these problems can be easily avoided by following the lessons in this book.

This book isn't just a training manual though. My aim is not only to give you some easy-to-understand training instructions but also to share my philosophy about dogs, and how I view their place in the home. I do this in the hope you will never be tempted to get rid of your dog because his behaviour has escalated beyond your control.

So to fulfil my promise to deliver my dog training as jargon (and bullshit) free as is humanly possible, I am going to start by teaching you the two laws you must learn and adhere to if you want to have a stress-free life with your new puppy.

The Law of the Dog

In 2016 I was lucky enough to interview dozens of amazing dog trainers from all over the world for my podcast, the Superhero Dog Owners Show, which is still available on iTunes. I listened to their stories and tried glean some of their wisdom to augment my own.

One phrase was mentioned time and time again, and was described most simply by fearful-dog specialist Debbie Jacobs, who said these four words.

"Dogs do what works".

That's kind of all you need to know about why dogs do the annoying things they do, and it also holds the key to how you are going to train your new puppy.

Here are a few examples:

- Dogs pull on the lead because it's gets them to the park quicker.
- Dogs run away to play with other dogs because it's fun.
- Dogs steal food from the kitchen counter because it tastes mighty fine.
- Dogs roll in fox shit because … OK, no one really knows why dogs roll in fox shit, but they obviously have their reasons, and they MUST enjoy it!

That's easy enough, right?

Dogs *do* what works.

Another way to put it would be to say dogs do what they enjoy doing, or what makes them happy.

I'll go into more detail about exactly how dogs learn in the next chapter, but for now, just remember dogs, and that includes puppies, **do what works**.

The next law I'm actually borrowing from one of my favourite writers, Robert Ringer, and it's his law of reality.

The Perfect Puppy Project

Robert contends the ultimate, immutable law of the universe is **Actions have consequences.**

This applies to every aspect of our lives:

Eat too much pizza, and you'll get fat.

Don't save or invest any of your wages, and you'll end up skint and pissed off in your old age.

Drive on the wrong side of the road without a seatbelt, and you'll probably crash and be killed.

This **law of reality** applies to directly to our dogs and puppies too.

If we know dogs are only willing do things they enjoy (and we *do* know because it's rule number one) then we can make life incredibly easy for ourselves by only allowing our puppies to enjoy things that we want them to do.

In Jordan Peterson's bestselling book *12 Rules for Life*, he states rule 5 is *"Do not let your children do anything that will make you dislike them"*.

Well, this rule can also be applied to your puppy, and you *shouldn't* allow your puppy to practise any behaviours you won't like them doing when they're an adult dog.

This means *stopping* your puppy from chewing items you would rather he didn't.

This means *stopping* your puppy from running away from you in the park.

This means *stopping* your puppy from pulling on the lead.

This means *stopping* your puppy from howling and crying when you have to leave him to go to work.

This means *not* allowing your puppy to run riot in your house, knock over Grandma and bite your kids' ankles.

"But, how do I do I stop all that, Dom!?!"

Fear ye not, dear reader; all is about to be revealed.

Just remember the two laws of dog training.

1. Dogs do what works.
2. Actions have consequences.

Keep those in mind and you will not only avoid becoming one of the unfortunate dog owners who end up giving up their difficult dog, but you will survive and thrive during this tricky puppy period and come out the other side with a new best friend who you can't live without.

So, without further ado, turn the page and let's begin chapter 1 with an explanation of purposeful puppy training.

The Perfect Puppy Project

Chapter 1
Purposeful Puppy Training

" … no good can ever come from spoiling a child like that, Charlie, you mark my words."

Grandpa Joe – Charlie and the Chocolate Factory by Roald Dahl

"Puppies!" Squuuuuuuuuuueeeeeeeeeeeeeeeeeel!!!!

So goes the high-pitched sound of every man, woman and child as soon as they see a brand new puppy. Me included.

If you look up cuteness in the dictionary you'll see it reads, *"the quality of being attractive in a pretty or endearing way"*, but a better description would be *"a nine-week-old puppy!"*

The Perfect Puppy Project

I mean, what's not to like?

The dopey eyes.

The Bambiesque legs.

The sweet-smelling paw pads.

The unspoiled softness of puppy fur.

I'm going all gooey-eyed just writing this stuff down.

It's all there for you to enjoy!

Well, for the 12 minutes your dog remains a cute little puppy anyway …

OK, 12 minutes may be a slight exaggeration, but it doesn't take long for your dainty little puppy to develop into a giant mass of clumsiness.

He's still lovable for sure, but soon the 'cute factor' evaporates, and what's left more resembles a normal pet dog.

If you really want to know how quickly the cute factor wears off, just see how other people react to your puppy as he grows bigger.

A 10-week-old puppy will get cooed at, praised and stroked when he stands up on his back legs as he attempts to get affection from a stranger.

But two months down the line, the same stranger will usually be a lot less keen to be trampled on by your clumsy pup, especially if you own a large breed with muddy paws.

The fact is, the puppyhood period (the first six months anyway) represent such a small part of your dog's overall life.

It can be as low as 1/36 for some long-living breeds.

So, before we dive into the training lessons, I would like you to have a think about exactly what kind of dog you want your puppy to become.

Personally, I want my dog to be:

- friendly, and certainly non-aggressive, but not too friendly with other people and dogs
- easy to exercise and control off lead
- happy to be left alone at home if I'm not there.

And if *you* want to enjoy a long, happy and stress-free relationship with your dog, then you should have similar wants.

This means from the moment you bring your puppy home from the breeder, almost everything you do with him needs to be a purposeful activity that will help him develop into the dog you desire.

Purposeful puppy training

Purposeful doesn't mean you need to be training your puppy all the time, or that you won't enjoy yourself, far from it. You'll have loads of fun following the programme I lay out in this book.

But because puppies are little sponges that quickly soak up all available knowledge, it's vital you <u>only allow</u> your puppy to practise behaviours that contribute to him being a well-behaved dog.

Practice makes perfect puppies, or does it?

They say practice makes perfect, but it depends what you're practising …

For example, you can't say one of your future goals is you want to be able to safely exercise your dog off lead in the park, but then allow your puppy to learn to enjoy chasing squirrels, pigeons and other dogs.

That's like me saying I really want to lose weight and get fitter, but then not doing any exercise and munching on cookies every time I walk into the kitchen. Those behaviours make it impossible (or at least incredibly difficult) for me to reach my goal of losing weight.

And similarly, if we want your puppy to be

1.   easy to exercise
2.   OK left home alone
3.   well socialised and non-fearful of most things …

… then the actions we take on a daily basis have to be in line with those goals.

Keep this in mind as you progress through the training. There is always a reason, usually a very good one, why I suggest what I do in this book. This shit works.

Before the puppy arrives

There's an ancient Japanese saying which goes *"the best time to plant a tree is 20 years ago. The second best time is now".*

Well, the best time to train your new puppy is the first time you bring him home, and if you didn't start then, the second best time is now.

I'm going to assume you have just acquired or will very soon be getting your puppy, so let me lay out a plan of action you can follow from the moment you bring him home.

Actually, let's take it back a step and quickly run though what you should do *before* you pick up your puppy.

There are lots of things you can do to puppy-proof your house which will make the first few days as stress free as possible.

Puppy-proofing your house

I read a newspaper article about teenage footballers who are talented and lucky enough to play for Premier League clubs. These kids are sometimes given £100,000 a week to kick a ball around.

I'm not jealous at all, *honest*.

But unless those young men are super grounded, and have a great support system in place, then it's probably not surprising some of them go a bit nuts when they progress from earning £300-£1,500 a week to £100,000. I don't know what the solution is to that particular problem but I do know you need to *avoid* giving your puppy too much, too soon.

If your puppy has easy and immediate access to all of the rooms, food, toys and affection he desires, then he will be excited, overwhelmed and really difficult to control.

And your puppy is going to be pretty excited anyway when he enters his new home, which is full of sights, smells and other interesting stuff.

He will need no invitation to sniff, lick and chew anything he can reach. You can help him get acclimatised *and* quickly settled in by <u>restricting what he has access to.</u>

Most inexperienced dog owners make the mistake of entering their home, and then putting the puppy down and letting him bugger off anywhere he wants in the house.

When I ask them why, they will say *"I need my puppy to explore his new home."*

To which I reply *"No, no, you don't."*

Your puppy only needs to explore and get used to the rooms he is going to be allowed in.

Preventing piles of indoor puppy poops

Another reason why you should NOT allow your puppy to 'explore' your house unsupervised is that you are simply going to prevent a lot of problems which would almost definitely occur if you give him free rein.

Your 10-week-old puppy has a curious mind, a mouth of razor-sharp teeth and a bladder the size of an egg cup. This means he is going to seek out and find things he can chew, and he's also going to pee very soon.

If you are controlling the environment and watching him carefully then you can pre-empt this and get your puppy outside for a pee before he finds a nice rug or a corner of the room to go in. This is almost impossible to do when he is flying from room to room as he pleases.

Preparing your children for your new puppy

Your children should be prepared before the puppy arrives and told how talk to and handle the puppy.

For the record, I'm not a fan of buying puppies as presents for kids, partners or anyone else. Trust me, if you're the one handing over the money for the puppy, then you are the one doing most of the work.

I know it's difficult with excitable kids, but try to keep craziness to a minimum, and certainly DO NOT allow young children to interact with your new puppy on their own.

Children have a different kind of energy and smell to adults, and puppies pick up on this. The puppy will see the excited child running around squealing as a fun person to be around and then chase them.

With the right supervision, your puppy and children will eventually bond well together, but remember, when you first bring him home your puppy has just come from living with his brothers and sisters, whom he is used to biting and roughhousing on the floor with.

Over the next few days you will teach your puppy not to bite and jump up at people, but for now the quickest way to stop your puppy from chasing and chomping bits out of your kids' limbs is to *not* let the kids run around in the first place, and closely supervise the interactions.

Other dogs and your new puppy

Controlling the family interactions also applies to any existing dogs you own, which you will obviously want your puppy to meet.

If you're adding a puppy to a household with a dog (or two) living in it already, there are a couple of canine commandments to adhere to:

1. It's not the older dog's responsibility to tell the puppy off when he's acting up and being annoying. That's <u>your</u> job. Or rather, it's your job to ensure you put steps in place to make sure your dogs end up living together in harmony.
2. Your dog's don't need to (nor should they necessarily) sleep and spend a lot of time together. A puppy that spends all of its time playing with, sleeping with and bonding with another dog will, in time, start to see that dog as its owner. Which means he won't listen to the actual owner, i.e. YOU, and he will just follow the other dog around instead.

Don't get me wrong, I can see the appeal of two cute dogs cuddling up in bed together, but then I also think about what will happen to the puppy if/when the older dog passes away, and I realise it's a good thing I make it a priority to teach my puppy to be OK sleeping, eating and resting ON HIS OWN. That way he will never become overly dependent on the older dog.

Let your new puppy live his own life, and don't saddle him with the handicap of never being able to enjoy any experience unless his older brother or sister is present.

Home checklist

So, a brief checklist for when you bring your puppy home.

Depending on how long you have driven your puppy home from the breeder's house it's a good idea to let your puppy down for a wee *before* you even enter your home.

So take him to the place you want him to 'go potty', 'pee' or 'get busy' (just some of the commands I've heard owners give their dogs) and let him go. Then it's time to carry your puppy over the threshold and enjoy your new life together.

Lead on Macpup

I'm a huge fan of using a house lead on a puppy. This is just a soft, short lead that you can use indoors to stop your puppy from jumping up at people or wandering where he shouldn't.

Think of it in the same way as one of those safety harnesses you would attach to a young child to stop them wandering off and getting lost in the supermarket.

Attach the lead to his collar (yes, you will go through a few collars over the next few months as your puppy grows) then put your puppy onto the floor and allow him to explore each room he's allowed into, one room at a time.

This can be quite overwhelming for your puppy, so really take your time, and if he lies down, or just seems tired, then make a brew and have 10 minutes with him chilling on the couch.

That's if you even want your puppy on the couch with you. There's a thing called a dog bed which your puppy will be extremely happy to lie in, if you teach him to lie in it. This is your call, but please DO NOT allow your puppy on the couch with you, and then complain when at six months old he jumps up and knocks your coffee out of your hand. And only the cruellest owner would encourage and allow their dog to sit on the couch with them, only to banish the dog from the settee when he is old and incontinent.

You need to keep the long game in mind when it comes to training your puppy.

How to tell when your puppy needs to 'go potty'

If when your puppy is wandering around he starts to look like he's searching for something but he can't remember where he left it, then he is usually looking for somewhere to pee (the other more obvious tell-tale sign if your puppy needs a number 2 is spinning on the spot with his bum pointing to the floor.) Don't worry though; you'll pick all these little signs up in the next few days.

As soon as you even suspect he needs to 'go' then just lead him outside, or pick him up and carry him out into the garden/yard area you have designated is going to serve as your pup's rest room.

We will cover housetraining in the next chapter, but for now just remember to keep taking him out regularly.

What is out of bounds for puppy?

Remember, your puppy only needs to go in the rooms he is going to spend time in.

He doesn't need to (nor should he) go upstairs. His small puppy joints aren't ready for it, and besides it's simply not safe for your puppy to travel up and down stairs unaccompanied. A child's stairgate fitted, even temporarily, can help you eliminate that problem and is a good investment to make.

How friends, relatives and children can safely meet and greet your puppy

Introductions and interactions with children and pets should be made with adult supervision.

Get your child to sit on the couch (yes, children can be taught to 'sit' too), then you sit beside them holding the puppy. The puppy will be curious in the child, and when he's had a sniff the child can say hello, give a stroke and introduce themselves to the puppy.

Once the puppy is comfortable, you can lift him onto the child's lap and assist them holding the puppy for themselves. Or, if your puppy is unsure and less confident, the child can use an open-arm invitation and allow the puppy to choose to approach or move away. When you are done you can lift the puppy off again.

Don't allow children to hug and squeeze the puppy too tightly. Just because you and your child like 'big hugs' doesn't mean to say your puppy will, yet. It can and does lead to growls and bites, so err on the side of caution until your puppy has settled in, and your child has settled down.

Calm interactions like that will hopefully be the starting point for a lifelong friendship between your new puppy and your children.

House rules

Your puppy doesn't care if he eats too much food, plays too aggressively or exercises too vigorously. He has no idea what consequences are; a lot of the time you have to *think* for him.

You need to guide and influence the puppy to make the correct decisions.

So start by deciding where your puppy is going to sleep. I would highly recommend your puppy sleeps in a crate. Crates are amazing inventions and will take a lot of the stress and mess out of raising your puppy. Crate training also plays a key role in the Play, Eat, Sleep, Repeat formula I teach in chapter 4.

And speaking of stress, mess and doggy distress, let's quickly look at the five most common puppy mistakes, which you need to avoid …

Big Fat Puppy Mistake Number One

The puppy is given too much freedom.

Using a crate effectively means your puppy can sleep in any room. He will be unlikely to wee or poo in the crate, so you can easily move it upstairs to your bedroom, which you might well want to do for the first night or two.

Then you should decide on a suitable 'bedroom' for your puppy. This is going to be his main 'rest room' and the place where he will spend a lot of time, especially when you spend extended periods of time out of the house, at work for example.

For that reason it might be a good idea for the puppy's main room to be somewhere away from the front door; so he won't easily see you leaving the house and going to work.

You can start to get him used to being alone now, by leaving him in his crate in his room, while you spend time in another part of the house.

Having his own room and rest area will be comforting for your puppy, and it will give you somewhere to put him when you have to take in a parcel, or pay the milkman.

Having his own room and restricting his access to other rooms will also prevent him from damaging furniture and other items, and from running upstairs, which is bad for his young puppy joints.

Big Fat Puppy Mistake Number 2

Teaching your puppy to have separation anxiety.

No, that isn't a typo. Many new puppy owners unwittingly teach their puppies to have separation anxiety.

Allow me to explain.

It's common for new dog owners to take a week or two off work so they can spend as much time as possible with their new addition. This is sensible as you will have some sleep-interrupted nights (because of the housetraining) and you will be spending a lot of time socialising your new puppy, as well as fun stuff like training, bonding and cuddling him too.

However, during the first few weeks he lives with you your puppy MUST be given time on his own so he doesn't become overly dependent on you being there.

Think of it from the puppy's point of view. If he hasn't spent a lot of time in his crate getting used to being by himself, he will feel like his world has ended when you go back to work, especially if you've spent every available minute with him for the last 7 to 14 days.

You can easily teach your puppy to be happy being by himself by regularly using just the crate, and enforcing lots of downtime.

Full instructions to *avoid* teaching your puppy to have separation anxiety are coming up.

Big Fat Puppy Mistake Number 3

<u>Telling your puppy off for doing something wrong.</u>

In case you hadn't guessed already, I'm not one of these fluffy-bunny, unicorn-fart-eating dog trainers who thinks you should never say no to a puppy. You absolutely should. Your puppy will quickly learn that "No" said in a low voice, accompanied by a furrowed brow, means he won't get anything good, and "Good boy" said in a happy voice coupled with a smiley face (and maybe a treat) means he is doing something good.

That's what we in the business call 'dog training'.

What you must avoid doing is telling your puppy off *after* he's done something you deem to be bad.

Puppies do naughty things all the time, and given half a chance they will poo on the floor, eat your slippers and pinch any food you leave within reach (although they will get into a lot less trouble if you control the environment and don't let them do those naughty things).

But mistakes still happen, and when your puppy does any of the above, or even something worse like ripping wallpaper off the walls, it's vital you *don't* tell him off afterwards.

How to avoid making your puppy fear you

When they've caught the dog 'in the act' a lot of owners tend to say something like *"he knows he's done wrong!"* (I know they do, because I've said it myself). The fact is, though, unless you catch the dog in the act then he doesn't know he's done wrong at all. He just knows you are pissed off at him, but he has no idea why.

See, dogs can't reason like us humans, and unless you have caught him in the act then your puppy won't know you are annoyed because he's chewed or pooed, and no amount of shouting or pointing at the offending item will make him understand. <u>So don't do it.</u>

The best thing to do when you discover your puppy has done something you don't like is to grab the nearest magazine or newspaper, roll it up like a truncheon and whack yourself over the head with it nine times, chanting this phrase:

I
Must
Not
Let
My

Puppy
Do
Silly
Things.

If your puppy pees on the floor or chews up your TV remote, it's your fault for not letting him out quick enough, or for leaving said remote where he could get easy access to it.

Don't worry though; you'll soon remember not to do it once you've hit yourself over the head a couple of dozen times.

Big Fat Puppy Mistake Number 4

Feeding your puppy from a bowl.

You can get crystal-embossed Versace bowls, aluminium clangers and plain old ceramics, but you won't be needing any of them, because for the first three months of his life you will be mainly feeding your puppy by hand, or from a food-dispensing toy.

Your puppy's food is a precious resource. Don't waste it by feeding him from a bowl. You can use it for training, for playing, for finding and for grooming. You can use food to help you bond and connect with your puppy, to teach him to walk to heel, and to do simple tricks which he will love learning, and you will *love* teaching him.

To 'use the food', though, you need to actually *use it*.

You want your puppy eager to work for food and to look to you as the provider. I'll go into much greater detail about how you can effectively 'use the food' in chapter 5.

Big Fat Puppy Mistake Number 5

<u>Failure to socialise the puppy.</u>

As we discussed in the prologue, once you bring your puppy home you have a matter of weeks to get him out into the big wide world, exploring and experiencing new sights, smells and sounds.

This is non-negotiable, I'm afraid.

Are you feeling tired because you just finished a tough shift at work, and you were up three times last night letting your puppy out for a wee?

Tough titty. Drink a Red Bull, and get outside and socialise him.

Is it raining and windy outside, and besides your puppy is so comfy and cute curled up on your lap?

Tough titty once again. You need to get grip of yourself, shove a coat on and get outside and socialise him.

Point well made, I hope.

Seriously though, your puppy MUST be properly socialised. Failure to take him out when you know you should (and you know you should because I'm telling you to) is tantamount to abusing him.

You are potentially setting him up for a lifetime full of fear *if* you don't adequately socialise him.

So how exactly do you go about socialising him? Well, socialisation deserves a chapter of its own, which you'll get to soon enough.

Summary

- Practise purposeful puppy training. This means only allowing your puppy to practise things you want him to do. If you don't want your puppy to wee on the floor or chew up your house, use a crate to prevent him from doing it. If you don't want your dog to run away from you in the park, don't let him chase bees, butterflies and birds into the distance when he's a puppy. *Be consistent.*

- Cards on the table time; being a responsible owner for your puppy can be bloody hard work. It's much easier to just cuddle your puppy all the time and let him do whatever makes him happy. But that's a sure-fire way to guarantee your puppy grows up to be a pain-in-the-arse dog who can never be left alone. With puppies you sometimes have to be a tiny bit cruel to be kind.

- The rules you put in place, and the effort you inject into your puppy's training now, will determine what kind of dog he turns into. Start by deciding what kind of dog you want to have. My suggestion is to go for a dog who is **Easy to exercise, OK to be left alone, Well behaved, Affectionate.** Your blueprint to achieve this goal begins in the next chapter …

BONUS – To help you get perfectly prepared for your puppy's arrival, I've come up with a Perfect Puppy Shopping List you can download. I can almost guarantee you'll end up getting too many soft toys more suitable for human babies, and not enough practical treat-dispensing toys to entertain your puppy and give him an outlet for his chewing habits. So if you want to get the essential items then download the shopping list at:

www.mydogssuperhero.com/perfectpuppyproject

Chapter 2

How Your Puppy Learns

"A puppy is but a dog, plus high spirits, and minus common sense".
Agnes Repplier

You will be familiar with the Hans Christian Andersen fairy tale about the ugly duckling.

The scruffy little duckling with his brown fledgling feathers was made fun of by all the other farm animals. He leaves the farm and suffers one hardship after another, until winter comes and he takes refuge in an old barn.

Then when spring arrives the duckling sees a flock of beautiful swans, and he throws himself at them believing it's better to be killed by such beautiful birds than to live a life of ugliness and misery.

He sounds like a real drama drake, doesn't he?

Anyway, to his surprise the swans welcome and accept him, and it isn't until he looks at his reflection in the water he realises he's grown into one of them and is now the prettiest swan of all.

Hurrah!

That's a story about personal transformation for the better. The little duckling started off life as an ugly chick, but in time developed into a handsome swan.

The *opposite* thing tends to happen with our puppies. They start off cute balls of fluff we can't get enough of but can soon develop into little monsters who terrorise the dog park and make our lives a misery.

At around one year old your puppy hasn't finished growing, but they are usually approaching full size, and they have certainly left behind the squishy-faced, cute puppy characteristics.

It's around this time they enter the 'teenage dirtbag' stage when they start to throw their weight around, push the boundaries and generally become little bastards.

This can be a challenging period for you the owner. But rest assured this stage soon passes, although not quick enough for some dog owners, who decide the puppy has changed for the worse and is not worth keeping. It's no coincidence nearly 40% of dogs who are given up for adoption are aged between seven months and one year.

To ensure you aren't among the unlucky puppy owners who end up getting rid of their dog, there are some things you need to know.

How to program your puppy

I like to use the computer hardware/software analogy when describing how your puppy learns, and it's my book, so that's what I'm going to do.

The hardware is the physical stuff in your computer, the electronic parts you can only change with a screwdriver or a soldering iron.

The software is the programs on it such as Microsoft Windows, Google Chrome or Minecraft. Then there is the firmware, which is the software the computer has built into it. This is a special kind of software not intended to be changed once the unit is shipped, and it cannot be erased.

Your puppy comes made up in a similar way.

You have the hardware of the dog: this is his physical make-up. There are many different 'models' to choose from, but all dogs essentially have the same physical characteristics.

Then there is the software, which is everything the puppy learns from the moment he's born. These inputs start at birth with what the puppy learns from his mother, such as how hard to bite his siblings when playing and when to eat. This then progresses to the housetraining, tricks and everything else *we* teach him once we get him home.

Finally you have the oft-forgotten firmware, which is the code embedded in your dog's DNA, which you can't erase.

This includes all the things that your dog wants and needs to do, even though no one taught him to do it, and which you'd much rather he didn't.

I'm talking about stuff like digging, chewing, hunting, herding and other breed-specific traits.

It's the software and the firmware you need to be most concerned about when you are training your puppy.

Fido's firmware

If you've bought a pointer or a vizsla then you can almost guarantee your dog is, at some point in his life, going to be interested in birds. Depending on how highly bred and driven he is will influence whether he wants to avoid, watch, smell, chase or hunt them.

The same is true of a collie dog, who will at some point in his life try herding you and your family up at the park like a pack of sheep, or a mastiff who will take great pride in guarding the house, or a terrier who likes nothing better than destroying a brand-new squeaky toy.

Those are examples of the breed-specific firmware of your dog. They are the breed characteristics already built into him, and which cannot be erased. What your dog is 'into' will differ slightly depending on whether you bought a gun dog, terrier, toy or guarding breed.

Then there's the more general firmware, which includes the activities that almost all dogs like doing, no matter what breed they are. This includes activities like playing, chasing, chewing and digging. In the next chapter I'll be showing you how to provide a safe and stimulating outlet for each of these activities from day one.

Then we come to the software, which is everything the puppy learns from the moment he is born.

Dogs learn by doing

Any activity which leads to a pleasant experience will more than likely be repeated by your dog. Receiving a treat and a pat on the head from you for doing a sit would be a good example of this.

The treat should be something that is rewarding for your puppy, and if your timing is good, and the treat is delivered very shortly after he's sat down then your puppy will be more likely to sit again next time you ask him.

But we aren't the only ones who can provide rewarding experiences for our dogs.

Your puppy can learn to like almost anything.

An example is when your puppy pinches food from the counter tops which you failed to push out of his reach. This may be annoying to you but pleasurable for him and so likely to be repeated in the future.

Conversely, any activities which lead to an unpleasant experience are likely to be avoided by your dog, so anything involving pain or fear will cause your dog to want to avoid it.

Cocker spaniel coffee mishaps

When my cocker spaniel Sidney was a puppy he accidentally put his foot in a hot cup of coffee. No lasting physical damage was done, but to this day if any of us bring a mug to our lips he will lean away and give us the 'whale eye'.

Whale eye in dogs is when they turn their head slightly and show the whites of their eyes. It's one way of telling you they are anxious and uncomfortable.

And the experience Sidney had is the same one resulting in so many dogs being terrified of fireworks.

How dogs learn to be afraid

If you got your puppy in January, then unless you introduce the sound of fireworks to him when he is very young, then it's quite possible the first firework he hears will be during a chilly evening walk in mid-October.

The offending firework screams into the sky then bangs, causing your dog to fill his pants. You console him as best you can, but often the damage is done, and it can be very difficult to comfort and rehabilitate a frightened dog. Don't worry though; I've got a whole section to ensure your puppy is totally fine with fireworks, hairdryers, bin lorries and anything else making a scary noise.

Remember what we learned earlier: **Dogs learn by doing**.

This mean activities your puppy finds rewarding and pleasurable will be eagerly repeated by him.

And unpleasant behaviours won't be repeated and may be avoided altogether.

All you need to do is keep giving your puppy rewarding and happy experiences that he wants to repeat, and avoid activities that make him feel uncomfortable and afraid.

We can easily do this with food, which is one of the main reasons I want you to feed by hand instead of from a bowl. Food is just one reward though, and I also want you to use affection, play and your emotions.

Training your puppy with food

Food is often the most commonly used training tool, and I have no problem with you using food to train your dog; in fact I positively encourage it.

Some trainers don't think you should use food to train your dog; they believe the dog should do something because he should instinctively want to please you. We have a name for those types of trainers. We call them arseholes.

The fact is you should use everything at your disposal to train your puppy. This includes toys, treats, games, tickles behind the ear, belly rubs, silly high-pitched cooing noises AND food.

What you don't want to do is turn into a treat-dispensing robot who just doles out food with no emotion involved. Most dogs are super motivated by food and will eat all day long, but some aren't turned on by food at all. And what happens if your puppy isn't hungry, or there is something more exciting on offer which can steal his attention away from you?

Then you need the *power of play*.

I discovered the power of play when I attended my first dog training intensive with dog training legend John Rogerson. I had recently started my own dog adventure company but quickly realised I knew nothing about dogs.

Not enough to keep good control of them anyway. John showed me how to influence and train a dog using my energy, personality and by finding and playing a game they liked. This became the basis of the play programme I teach in my bestselling *How To Be Your Dog's Superhero* book, which has helped thousands of dog owners all over the world, and it forms the basis of your relationship with your new puppy.

So by using food, affection, emotion and play to reward him, your puppy will quickly learn what is expected of him.

What gets rewarded gets repeated

Any pleasurable experience your puppy has is likely to be repeated, and even sought out by him. The key here is to remember it's what your puppy finds pleasurable that will be repeated, *not* what you want him to enjoy.

If you've owned a dog before you will know they can enjoy some pretty disgusting things, and if you haven't owned a dog before then you are in for quite a shock. Dogs like everything from drinking stagnant water to rolling in (and even eating) dog shit or rotting animal carcasses. Fortunately, it's possible to stop your puppy doing any of those disgusting things with a marvellous invention called a dog lead.

This brings me to the second crucial learning point many new dog owners (and some dog trainers) seem to forget, and it is this:

Your puppy is always learning.

Whenever he's awake your dog is constantly taking in what's going on around him, and when he's asleep he is processing the information. That's called latent learning and we humans do a similar thing; this is one reason why it's good to give your dog little breaks when you are training him so he can process what just happened.

Puppies are also very curious creatures, and their inquisitive nature can get them into a lot of trouble.

For example, we know all dogs like to chew, and we further know puppies are especially prone to chewing; they do this for many reasons but mainly because dogs just like chewing. Much like babies, puppies will put almost anything in their mouth, and when their needle-like teeth are cutting, they demand to be soothed and comforted with a suitable chew toy.

Of course a suitable chew toy for your puppy is anything he can get his jaws round. TV remotes, Kindle and iPhones have all been used as expensive chew toys in chez Hodgson. Why? Because I failed to remember my puppy is always learning, and so my first puppy learned to chew whatever I gave him access to. The introduction of a crate gave me control of the environment and meant my puppy could only 'learn' to chew what I left in his crate, i.e. dog chews and toys!

Your puppy can also learn to pull on the lead, bark at the postman, jump up and annoy guests, and chase leaves that float by, and he probably *will* learn to do all those things unless you teach him something else.

What gives you the edge in this ongoing battle as your puppy develops is you control the environment.

The Perfect Puppy Project

Are you a teacher, trainer, friend or puppy parent?

The fact is, you are all of the above, and you get to decide whether to let your puppy rest in a crate, or whether to give him the run of the whole house. And whether to allow him to graze on his food whenever he's peckish, or to instead use his food as a reward so you can influence and train him.

You get to decide whether to take toys and treats to the park to play with your puppy while he's attached to a long lead, or whether to allow him free rein to do whatever he likes.

And if you haven't been paying attention, let me tell you it's the former you should be practising each time with your dog. The more you control the environment and teach your puppy all good things come from you, the better behaved, easier to control and more enjoyable he will be.

This brings me nicely onto socialisation.

The socialisation problem

Socialisation is a much misunderstood concept among dog owners (and some dog trainers too).

Socialisation is so important because of the ticking clock that starts when you bring your puppy home.

A lot happens in the first 12 weeks of a puppy's life. It reminds me of a time-lapse photography video, where they take a still photograph each day of a plant growing and blooming into flower, then they speed the film up so you can watch several days or weeks of footage in a few seconds.

Let's have a quick overview of the fast-track development all puppies go through from the moment they are born.

Neonatal – birth to two weeks

As you would imagine puppies can't do a lot when they first leave the womb. They can taste and touch, but their ears, eyes and nose don't kick in until week two or three. They rely on the mother for everything. She provides heat to warm them, nuzzles for comfort, feeds them and licks their rude bits to stimulate bowel or bladder movement, and then eats what comes out. Yuck. And you thought changing nappies was gross!

Transitional stage

Next comes the transitional stage. This is where is all starts kicking off in the pen. Well, not really but there's a lot more activity occurring now. Your puppy's eyes open and he begins to stand, sit, wag his tail and play with his siblings.

From week four onwards your puppy gets quite active and strong. He will move away from the sleeping area to do his toileting (but the male dogs will forget to put the seat down).

By week five he will look and act like a proper little dog (see, I *told* you it was a fast process). He will be playing and rolling around with his brothers and sisters, and enjoying the toys the breeder has left in the pen. His mother will teach him not to bite her (or the other pups) too hard.

The Perfect Puppy Project

By week six your puppy is piling the weight on. Anything from 5 ounces to 2.5 pounds depending on the breed, and the breeder should be introducing the puppy to lots of new experiences each day.

By the end of week seven some puppies may be leaving the nest to join their new home, and by week eight this operation will be in full swing. The mother will continue to teach him bite inhibition when she visits him to play.

Then you come along and take your puppy away from everything he's ever known and place him in a completely new environment, with new people and a whole new routine. Don't feel bad about this though; that's what supposed to happen. Your puppy is ready for the next chapter in his development.

By week nine your puppy will be living in his new home and acclimatising to his new surroundings, and you will be in full socialisation mode. This means you will be giving your puppy new experiences, and teaching and training him new behaviours every single day.

You will have noticed during the first eight weeks with his mother and siblings, the puppy did a lot of playing and biting, which his mother supervised and scolded him for if he got too carried away. That's her job. Your puppy plays with his siblings and the mother supervises. For the first eight weeks he is essentially learning how to be a dog.

When you pick him up he has officially graduated from 'learning to be a dog' school. Your puppy's dog-to-dog play education is finished, and done with. There is no need nor should you want him to play with other puppies or dogs anymore.

This goes against the grain of what many dog trainers will teach. They allow and many will even encourage puppies to play with one another in their classes. I believe this is unnecessary and potentially quite damaging to your puppy's development.

Until eight weeks old your puppy is effectively at doggie primary school. He's learning how to be a dog, and be with other dogs.

But from the minute you bring him home, *you* are teaching him how to be a 'pet dog', hopefully a great pet dog.

Part of this is teaching him to enjoy being with you, which means not allowing him to learn to love doing things that will make him difficult to look after.

Why your puppy doesn't need a million doggy friends

Think of a tadpole turning into a frog. When a tadpole is born it lives completely underwater and has more in common with a fish than a frog. Then it grows front and back legs, and gradually takes on the form of a frog, until its gills disappear and its lungs have enlarged when it's ready to leave the water.

Now a fully fledged frog, it has no need nor the capability to be a tadpole.

Well, your puppy's development works in a very similar way. Once he's left his mother and siblings he has no need to play with dogs ever again.

Can your puppy play with dogs?

Absolutely he can. If allowed and encouraged to do it, then playing with other dogs will be your puppy's favourite thing in the world.

But socialisation *isn't* about making sure dogs play nicely together. Ideally, you want your puppy to be no more interested in another dog than he is in a car, horse or lollipop man who helps the kids cross the street.

Imagine if every time you walked past a lollipop man he threw a tasty bit of steak for your puppy. How many times would that have to happen before your puppy realised lollipop men were there just to provide the tastiest treats for your puppy?

Answer: not many times at all.

After a while, your puppy would start looking for lollipop men and women when you took him for a walk, and when he saw one in the distance he would pull to get to them. Then he'd start whining, and eventually, if allowed to escalate, this frustration at not being allowed to get what he wants could lead to barking and aggression.

Sounds a bit dramatic?

Well, it *isn't*.

In my experience, far too many dog trainers have an idealistic yet unrealistic view of the world. They think pet dog owners have as much time as they do to train and play with their dogs. So they think a bit of harmless dog play is nothing to worry about.

But your average pet dog owner (and I'm assuming you are an average pet dog owner) only has a limited amount of time each day to exercise their dog, and if every time you take him to the park, or a puppy class, you allow your puppy to learn the most enjoyable thing there is playing with another dog, you are setting yourself up for a lifetime of stress and anguish.

I've seen dozens of dogs who are a nightmare to walk, and who the owners struggle to let off lead purely because they allowed their puppies to become too obsessed with playing with other dogs.

If you want your puppy to grow into an easy-to-manage, well-behaved dog who follows you around the park like you're the Pied Piper, then you need to be the source of his fun and entertainment and NOT other dogs.

Why am I so anti-dog-play? Because I've seen with my own and my clients' dogs how easy it is to lose control and ruin a dog by allowing them to become too interested in and to enjoy roughhousing and chasing other dogs.

Remember how dogs learn. They experience something pleasurable and enjoyable, which they will seek out and want to do again.

Well, if the most enjoyable thing your dog does at a puppy party is rolling around on the floor with other dogs then that is the thing he will remember and want to do again.

The same thing will happen if you allow your puppy to think the sole reason for going to the park is to run around with other dogs. That becomes the activity he will associate with 'going to the park'. This means he will not only look forward to going back to the park to chase and play with another dog, but if there is one in the distance he will likely run off to get to him.

This is about more than just socialisation. It's a philosophical stand you have to take.

I urge you to ignore the dog whisperers, *and* the fluffy-bunny trainers who live on Planet 'Make believe', and instead listen to your Uncle Dom.

If you teach your puppy all the entertainment, fun and stimulation in his life comes from you then you won't need to invest in training classes, clickers or even a dog lead. Well, maybe just a dog lead to get your dog safely to and from the park, but that's it.

So how do you teach your puppy you're the centre of his universe? It starts from the moment you bring your puppy home from the breeder.

Summary

- Think of your dog like a computer made up of hardware, software and firmware. The hardware and firmware you can't really change; these are the breed-specific traits that all dogs possess but which are most evident in gundogs, terriers and herders. However, you do get to program the software in your puppy. This means you can allow him to safely enjoy his breed-specific activities, if you provide a safe outlet for his desire to chase, hunt and play. And you can easily do this by playing games using toys and food.

- Socialisation is much misunderstood and the vast majority of dog owners get it horribly wrong. Correct socialisation is about getting your dog used to behaving in a calm and confident manner in all the everyday situations he is going to be exposed to later in life. This means gradually exposing your young puppy to new sights, sounds, smells and situations. It doesn't mean teaching him to play with other dogs. Trust me, if you want to enjoy long off-leash walks, trips to the pub and holidays with your dog then the last thing you want him doing is thinking it's playtime when he sees another dog.

- Your job is to convince your puppy you are the provider of all the food and fun he enjoys, and you are the person who will keep him safe and free from fear in all new situations. The stronger the bond you have with your puppy, the more he will look to you as his teacher, leader, parent and friend. You start to build that bond from the moment you pick him up, so in the next chapter let's look at the routine you need to follow from day one with your new puppy.

Chapter 3

Your Puppy's First Day

"The most important day of a person's education is the first day of school, not Graduation Day."

Harry Wong

A few times when I've been abroad we've had an evening flight which meant we arrived in the middle of the night when it's pitch black. This means I've been unable to see exactly what the hotel and surrounding area is like, until morning.

There's a certain amount of excitement and trepidation when you wake up in a strange hotel bed and peer out of the curtains to see if you've landed in paradise or a total shithole.

These days, of course, we have the benefit of Google Maps, t'internet and travel agent brochures to give us a better idea of where we are going.

But imagine being a puppy who is plucked from the litter, and then whisked away and dumped in a new home, where he knows nothing and no one.

Puppies are quite resilient and confident little critters who can and do adapt to new surroundings quite quickly, but I would like you to make the transition to his new home as easy and enjoyable as possible for your new puppy.

This means ideally you want to pick your puppy up in the morning, or certainly no later than midday – this gives you most of his first day to get to know each other.

An early morning pickup allows you to really take your time with the whole settling-in process. It means you can start the bonding with your puppy, and he has a whole day to get used to his brand-new home and family.

You are going to do so many fun things with your puppy over the next couple of months, and while you don't need to start everything straight away, it's nice if your puppy can go to bed in his new home having met everyone in the family, eaten some food, played a while and done a couple of wees outside.

Trust me on this; if you can collect your puppy earlier in the day, do it.

Your puppy's homecoming routine

There are a few key activities I like a new owner to get checked off the list in the first couple of hours your puppy arrives home.

The homecoming routine:

1. Meet everyone who lives in the house. This includes other pets. This doesn't mean to say the puppy has to be everyone's best friend from the first minute, but he should at least be introduced/shown to each family member.
2. Have a wee, outside. Puppies are actually pretty predictable when it comes to peeing. You just need to remember to take them outside after every play session, meal, treat, drink, introduction to new family member. Basically, if you ever catch yourself thinking *"Will my puppy need a wee now?"* then for dog's sake, take him. I guarantee if you don't, then *that* will be the time he pees or poops behind the settee.
3. Eat and drink something. I find dogs and puppies who are afraid or unsettled in some way don't tend to eat and drink, so it's nice if you can get your puppy to eat a little bit of food and have a drink. This is not difficult to do if you follow the Play, Eat, Sleep, Repeat formula I lay out in chapter 4.
4. Spend some time in the crate. It's mega tempting (and hugely enjoyable) to spend all your time cuddling your new puppy, but it's way more sensible to let your puppy spend at least some time in his crate BEFORE bedtime. So once your puppy has explored, played and eaten then he can spend a bit of time in his crate. This is something we do with the puppy and adventure dogs that home board with us. They get some fun and playtime, a nice meal and cuddles, but they ALSO get some time alone in the room we have designated their

bedroom. This means when bedtime comes around I'm not asking the dog to suddenly settle somewhere he's never been before.

You may be lucky and your breeder started crate training, but it's unlikely. Either way, you can start right away with my foolproof crate training plan.

Why crates are great

In time your puppy will see the crate as a cool place to chill out, but at first he may be, quite understandably, *not* so keen to go into the crate.

This is where the T-shirt or tea towel you hopefully brought from the breeder's home comes in really useful.

Place the T-shirt inside the crate, and this will reassure the puppy somewhat and provide a nice bridge between his old home and his new one. Placing some interesting chew toys in the crate will also give him something to do and may even encourage him to want to spend time in there.

How much sleep does your puppy need?

Answer: <u>a lot.</u>

The Disney trash-collecting robot WALL-E charges up with sunlight, but puppies charge up and indeed do most of their growing when they are sleeping. Your puppy should be tired after his journey home, but a bit of playing on the floor should be enough to deplete your puppy's energy reserves so he feels tired, then you can pop him in his crate with a KONG and let him chew himself to sleep.

Bingo, you've just started the crate training process and made the upcoming bedtime routine a lot easier to manage.

Remember, your puppy will probably need the toilet as soon as he wakes up. He won't want to wee or poop in his bed area, so as soon as he starts stirring, but *before* he starts crying to be let out, you can pop his collar and lead on and lead him outside to the toilet area.

When I say toilet area I don't mean the outside netty. I mean the place you have designated the outdoor area your puppy is going to wee and poop in. This can be a concreted area of your yard or a small patch of garden you don't mind going a bit yellow.

You can, of course, let him have the whole run of the garden, but I wouldn't recommend it. Far better to just lead your puppy outside (make sure you have a pair of wellies, a hat and a raincoat by the back door, or flip-flops in summer that you can quickly pull on). You are going to be doing a LOT of toilet breaks with your puppy in the next couple of weeks, so get prepared now.

Puppy peeing outfit checklist

- Wellies/flip-flops
- Poo bags
- An umbrella or waterproof coat (for you, NOT your puppy …)
- A treat (to reward your puppy for pooping outside)

Teaching your puppy to pee outdoors

Sometimes when you first take a puppy outside he won't wee straight away. Don't read too much into this; it's not because he is shy or embarrassed about the size of his puppy tinky.

It's just this is a brand new place to him, and he doesn't have any frame of reference for this new puppy piss-stop.

See, until now he's known where to pee because he could smell his own and his mother's pee. In your garden there's nothing but worm farts and dandelions. So you just have to be a little patient.

Encourage your puppy to toilet but don't worry about adding a command yet until your puppy is weeing regularly. You can jolly him along but please don't hassle your puppy to pee. In fact, ignoring him can work wonders because then he will be encouraged to sniff, which usually stimulates toileting.

This is another reason you should have a special 'toilet area' because once your puppy goes outside and wees in the toilet area, his scent will stay there for a long time. It will certainly be there the next time you take him outside; then your puppy will smell his own wee, which will encourage him to go again.

Once he's done this five or six times, and you've remembered to reward and praise him for doing so, then the habit is set and your puppy should wee and poop in the same spot every time you take him out.

Puppy's first night

Most owners find the first night with the puppy quite challenging, and there's a very good reason why. The first night with your new puppy can be *really* challenging!

Think about it for a second. Your puppy has been taken away from everything he associates with home, his mother, his siblings, his breeder and any family he had, plus all his usual toys and home comforts.

And you've had a busy day too, running around after him, supervising interactions, feeding, playing and cleaning up. That's not to mention the 45 times you've taken him out for a wee!

So a lot has happened today for both you *and* your puppy. He will be tired, and you will be tired *and* a little fraught (especially if you have other dogs or kids to add to the equation).

But if you have followed the homecoming plan until now, then you will have set your puppy up perfectly to settle in his crate until morning.

Your puppy's night-time routine

Ideally your puppy will have spent a good few hours off and on resting and sleeping in his crate throughout the day. This means even at this early stage he will be starting to associate being in the crate with sleeping or resting.

I'm stressing how important the 'tiredness factor' can be because I don't want you to put all this work in, and then by the time bedtime comes round, you are too tired to put your puppy in his crate and just think *"Stuff it, he can sleep in our bed tonight …"*

No, he can't!

Where should your puppy sleep on his first night?

In his crate of course, but you can move the crate around.

With my own most recent puppy, I did manage to leave him in his crate downstairs the whole night on his first night with us. After a little initial whining he slept until morning, with maybe one or two toilet breaks during the night.

But I also think it's perfectly fine to move the crate into your bedroom or the hallway outside your bedroom so your puppy can hear you.

Remember, this is his first night away from his siblings, his mother and the family who raised him, so at best he's going to feel a little displaced, and at worst he will be stressed and worried.

This is why we put a towel, a blanket or a T-shirt with traces of his mother's scent into the crate with him. Your puppy's nose is always open and he will recognise the smell, which he should find comforting.

Then if your puppy is near your bed, or just outside your bedroom, he will be able to hear and smell you, and you can reassure him with a few calming words that everything is OK.

Then you can start edging the crate further away each night until after a few days he will be downstairs in his permanent sleeping quarters.

No bedtime story required

You can make it easier for your puppy to settle on his first night by having a good old play session before bedtime. Nothing too strenuous, but you *are* trying to 'take the edge' off him before you retire for the evening.

Of course, all this depends on what your own puppy is like. Almost all puppies sleep a lot, but some come to our homes more full of beans than others.

If possible you want to try to get your puppy into the routine you want him to be in for the rest of his life. So as tempting as it is to lie in front of the TV all night with your puppy on your lap, ask yourself: is that the best way to get him used to sleeping and being happy in his crate? No, is the only sane answer.

Midnight wee-wees

As I said before, toilet training begins the moment you step through your front door, and it continues into the night too, especially for the first week or two.

At first your puppy has no way of regulating when he needs to 'go potty'; he simply feels the need and then goes.

But there are certain areas he won't want to wee in, and one of those is his bed. This doesn't mean he *won't* wee in his bed, he will *if* left for too long, but he won't *want* to, and he will wait until he's out of the bed/crate before he goes. This means you need to provide an opportunity for him to 'go' during the night.

If you are a light sleeper and usually get up to pee yourself at a certain time in the night, then after you've gone I would wash your hands (obviously) and then take your puppy outside for a wee.

Or if you sleep like the dead then you may need to set an alarm to take your puppy outside at least once during the night. Don't rely on you hearing your puppy crying when you are asleep, especially if he is downstairs in his crate; you won't!

Remember, your puppy doesn't want to wee in his crate, but he will *if* he has no other option. If he pees in the crate it's your fault for not letting him out. *Not* your puppy's fault.

And yes, night-time wee-wees mean you will have to put on your outdoor wee-wee outfit at 3 o'clock in the morning, but this is a small price to pay for a housetrained puppy, which is what you will own in few weeks' time, IF you stick to the plan.

Puppy pads

Are great for cleaning up spilled coffee or wine, but I'm not a fan of using them once you've brought your puppy home from the breeder's.

There may be some occasions when they are necessary, like if you lived in a flat and it was more difficult for you take your puppy outside, but in general I would recommend you stick to the plan as above.

The whole point of housetraining is to get your puppy to toilet outside the home. Puppy pads simply add an extra unnecessary step to the process.

That's day one done and dusted. Give yourself a paw on the back, and get an early night because tomorrow the fun really starts …

Summary

- You can make the transition from the breeder's to your home as pain free as possible by picking up your puppy in the morning. Take the day off if need be, but don't tell your extended family and friends. Let your puppy get used to his new home and your immediate family for 24 hours. Then you can spend a bit of quality time together getting to know each other. There will be a few hiccups and accidents but you'll have lots of happy memories of this special time together.

- Remember though, just because you *can* spend all day cuddling your puppy, it doesn't mean you *should*, and your puppy should spend at least an hour in the morning and afternoon settling or sleeping in his crate. He will be glad of the rest, and it will give you a chance to catch your breath and prepare him for the night-time routine. How quickly he settles in his crate at bedtime very much depends on the crate work you do with him during his first day in his new home.

- Housetraining starts from the moment you bring your puppy home. One of the biggest mistakes new owners make is in underestimating how often they should be letting their new puppy outside for a toilet break. The answer is to let him out all the time. Every half an hour at first, and always after he's had a drink, a meal, some treats, a play or training session and straight after a visitor has arrived. I've come up with a formula to enable you to crack the crate training code, which is what I will teach you in the next chapter.

BONUS – To help make the first few days with your puppy as easy and stress free as possible I've put together a Puppy Primer Audio Training which you can listen to at home or on the go, from your phone, computer or tablet. In this two-hour bonus training I pick out the key points from the book and give case study examples to show you how to quickly settle your new puppy into a routine.

To access this free bonus training, go to:

www.mydogssuperhero.com/perfectpuppyproject

<u>Chapter 4</u>

Your Perfect Puppy Formula

"My husband and I are either going to buy a dog or have a child. We can't decide whether to ruin our carpets or ruin our lives."

Rita Rudner

There's a moment when you bring your puppy home for the first time when you have a mini panic attack and immediately regret getting the dog. Usually you keep it to yourself and don't tell anyone, but we are four chapters in now, and I feel like we are becoming friends, so let's be honest with each other.

This feeling of regret soon passes, but the fact it's there, even just for a fleeting second, only emphasises that getting a puppy can be terrifying.

You are flying blind without a co-pilot, and the potential to crash and burn is never far away.

This is why it's crucial you set some 'house rules' for you, your family and your puppy to live by.

A lot of avoidable problems occur because inexperienced (or cocksure) new puppy owners don't set enough rules from the start. But as we learned in the Introduction, actions have consequences and the consequence of not giving your puppy any boundaries means he will do annoying and dangerous things.

My house, my rules

When my eldest son, Alex, was six we held a birthday tea party at our home for a few of his friends. I know, huge mistake, and we never repeated it again, but we were young, daft and didn't know any better.

It was like a scene from *Planet of the Apes*. His friends descended like a troop of manic monkeys and proceeded to blow through the house like a whirlwind, climbing all over the furniture, the couch and the stairs, stopping only to eat ice cream, pick their noses or go to the toilet.

After about 10 minutes I knew I needed to stop the chaos or go to the pub, and as the pub wasn't open and Beth was giving me 'the look', I settled for stopping the madness.

This was my house after all, and our Alex didn't usually act the way some of these kids were acting. Surely they didn't go on like this in their own homes? Surely their parents had rules for behaviour, just as we did for Alex?

Well, whether it was a lack of rules or an overload of sugar I didn't care; the shenanigans had to stop.

So I politely told them all to settle the fuck down or they would be going home early. I'm kidding of course; what I actually said was *"In this house we don't jump on the settee; we sit on it. And climb the stairs is just a figure of speech; in this house we just walk up and down the stairs. The banister is there to help you keep balance; it's not a parkour challenge."*

Sure enough, with some simple rules in place a quiet calm quickly descended, and now I'm left with (mainly) fond memories of Alex's first birthday party.

Puppy rules

Whoever said *"Rules are made to be broken"* clearly never had a puppy *or* hosted a kids' tea party, and having a set of rules in place before you get your puppy is crucial to the future harmony in your household.

Not everyone agrees with rules.

Mention the word 'rules' in front of fluffy-bunny dog trainers who are members of the puritanical positive people's front, and they will spit on the floor and call you a barbaric owner.

They argue only harsh, uncaring and unskilled dog trainers have any need for rules. They would rather you ask for your dog's permission before you make him do anything.

This is a classic example of seeing the world as you wish it to be. However, you and I live in the real world, and so we must see things as they actually are, and the simple fact is dogz needz rulez.

Why dogs need rules

This doesn't mean to say dogs necessarily want rules. Just like children they may resent and even rebel against some of the rules you put in place, but rules they need, and it starts the moment you bring your puppy home.

The big mistake novice dog owners make is they think rules mean consequences and so you are going to have to start beating your dog with a rolled-up newspaper whenever he does something wrong.

Don't worry; you aren't.

Phew.

There will be some consequences for your puppy for sure, but they won't be painful, scary or in any way damaging to him.

Why rules are necessary

There are different kinds of rules in life.

Rules prevent chaos and keep everyone operating on the same level. They give us an acceptable, uniform level of behaviour to aim for.

Some rules keep us safe, like rules for the road. Speed limit rules stop us from driving too fast, or overtaking when it's dangerous to do so.

Other rules are more habit forming. So when we are children the rules are to clean your teeth before you go to bed, or eat your vegetables or you won't get any dessert.

Those kind of rules help form the good habits that keep us healthier and prevent us having smelly breath.

Your puppy rulebook

A big difference between puppies and children is you can't reason with a puppy.

You can't sit him down and tell him a certain behaviour is unwanted in your house.

You can try doing that, by all means, but I don't think it's going to be a very productive chat.

The main reason you can't retrospectively explain things to a puppy (and let's conveniently skip over the first reason, which is you can't speak dog) is a lot of those activities are inherently rewarding for your puppy.

He *likes* eating food (even if it's stolen).

And he likes biting and chewing things (even if they are expensive items which you love dearly).

I'm not a dog so I can't say whether they particularly enjoy pooing and weeing, but we know those are biological necessities, so we can safely assume that like us puppies feel relief after they have gone to the loo.

You get the idea, I hope.

Because your puppy is pre-programmed to enjoy certain things this almost means he is pre-programmed to be annoying, messy and destructive.

So how do you stop this from happening? By employing the greatest dog training invention since the dog lead: the dog crate!

And to help you get the maximum benefit, I've invented a foolproof formula to help you get the best use out of your dog crate. And the formula is:

Play, Eat, Sleep, Repeat.

Play. Puppies love to play so you can tire him out and start building a great bond by playing with him. This, supplemented with short walks and trips into the garden, will be more than enough exercise for your puppy.

Next comes **EAT.** Puppies are hungry little beggars so you can make his meals last a lot longer and give him a good challenge by giving him some tasty KONGs to enjoy while he is in the crate.

Sleep. Then with a full tummy he will probably sleep off his food and dream of the next play session, which can happen a few hours later when you start the whole thing again and …

Repeat. Most puppies will accept and adjust to this routine really quickly. Then as they grow and need less sleep you can add more exercise, play, training and KONGs.

The stress-free formula

A routine like this makes it super easy for someone else to look after your puppy too. Make no mistake, you will need someone to help you look after your puppy when you go on holiday, work late or have a change in circumstances. And whether it's a friend, neighbour, relative or pet professional, you will find it easier to get someone to help you *if* your puppy is easy to look after and low maintenance, which he will be if you follow the Play, Eat, Sleep, Repeat formula.

By using this formula you are putting a routine in place that will help fix lifelong habits in your puppy. Then whoever is looking after him should be able to play, feed and put your puppy to sleep exactly the same way you do.

The consistency commandments to create a contented canine

You can start this routine the first day you bring your puppy home. I do have a heart, and I appreciate you are going to want to spend as much time as possible cuddling your puppy. However, you can start introducing the P.E.S.R. (Play, Eat, Sleep, Repeat) routine on day one, by ensuring your puppy spends at least *some* time sleeping and resting in his crate.

This routine is certainly going to help with housetraining, as it directs you when to take your puppy for a wee.

If members of your family are in and out of the house all day, then it might be an idea to keep a chart on the fridge and mark it with the last time puppy was out for a wee. That way even if your son/daughter/hubby/cousin/friend is with the puppy for an hour, they can stick to the schedule, let the puppy out for a wee at the appropriate time and so contribute to the housetraining process.

Your housetraining routine

Ideally you should take your puppy for a toilet break at each and every step of the P.E.S.R. routine. In fact, you should give your puppy the opportunity to toilet ALL the time, and definitely after he has done anything that involved him moving around.

So after you have been playing or training, or feeding him, or when someone arrives to visit, or after they leave. Whenever you think he *might* need a wee, take him for a wee.

This might seem like overkill but it really does work. If you don't allow your puppy to wee inside by ensuring he is outside more often than not, then you almost crack housetraining in a month or two, maybe even less.

The long game

We get so wrapped up in loving and cuddling our new puppy, it's easy to forget what our long-term needs (as owners) are going to be.

For example, if you get a puppy around December or January then he is unlikely to hear a firework until he is eight to 10 months old, which is slap bang in the middle of the second fear stage all puppies go through.

If you live in a built-up area where fireworks are common, then you'll have a difficult job of calming your puppy down.

So as soon as possible you need to start preparing your puppy for things he might not see for another six months, and the most obvious of these is fireworks.

Proofing your puppy for fireworks

You can get access to firework noises on YouTube, but I highly recommend my good friend Amy Smith's **Sound Proof Puppy App** (available on iTunes or Android phones). It is packed full of all the noises you want your new puppy to get used to, such as lawn mowers, drills, aeroplanes, bin lorries, even babies crying, and also fireworks.

Once you've downloaded the app, or wherever you've got the fireworks noises from, start by turning the volume down very low (the lowest) and play each sound while your puppy is asleep in his crate, or chewing a KONG after a walk or play session.

Gradually increase the volume by one bar each day, and with a week or two your puppy will be unfazed by any squealing babies or firecrackers that come from your phone.

It's a similar procedure getting your puppy used to being OK when left on his own too. And I'm *not* just talking about avoiding separation anxiety.

Preparing your puppy for holidays

If you intend going on holiday ever (and why wouldn't you?) then it would help if your puppy had been exposed to the stress of staying in a stranger's house from an early age.

Using a crate makes it much easier for your puppy to settle in someone else's house, as you are essentially taking the immediate bubble of his sleeping environment to the stranger's home, so the house will be strange but the sleeping bubble will *not* be.

There's always a little extra we can do. My first dog training mentor, John Rogerson, recommended leaving your puppy with a friend or relative for the odd night a couple of times within the first six weeks that you have him. This makes perfect sense when you think about it, but hardly anyone ever does this.

A good halfway house could be to take your puppy (and his crate) to a friend's or relative's house for an afternoon. This is an excellent way to start exposing your puppy to new environments.

When to start the routine

Once you've got the excitement of day one out of the way, you can begin getting your puppy acclimatised to his Play, Eat, Sleep, Repeat routine.

Here's a typical example of what day two (and days three, four and five) would look like.

You wake your puppy up, or as is more likely he wakes you up …

He goes straight outside to his toilet area for a wee.

You make a brew and then join your puppy on the floor, where you can play a game with him and practise your tummy rubs.

Then your puppy can go back into the crate while you go and get ready.

Once you are showered and shaved (female readers maybe just stick to the shower) then you can take him for a short walk, or a socialisation session outdoors if your puppy still hasn't finished his inoculations.

Then practise a few tricks indoors before you give him another opportunity to have a wee, and then pop him in his crate with a tasty kibble-filled KONG and a few chew toys.

So the crate makes it easy to enforce some rest or sleep time into your puppy's routine.

Summary

- Using a crate to manage your puppy is going to pre-vent a lot of unwanted chewing, weeing, pooing and overexcitement. In time your puppy will come to love his 'safe place', and if you wish you can use the crate indefinitely. My cocker spaniel, Sidney, is eight years old and still sleeps in his crate. The crate came in very useful when he unfortunately did his cruciate ligament and needed three months' crate rest. I dread to think how I would have coped without the crate.

- In the coming months you can adapt the Play, Eat, Sleep, Repeat formula to suit your own needs, but for the first few days use it as a guide to help you manage your puppy. Puppies love to play, and after a play ses-sion they will usually be hungry and tired, which means they will eat and sleep, and it's the sleeping they should do in the crate. You can structure his day and enforce much-needed downtime by sticking to the formula. He may not like it at first, but he will become

a better dog in the future because of the tough decisions you are taking now.

- Puppies need a lot of rest, whether they want it or not,
and they will spend the majority of the day sleeping in
their crate. But 'Sleep' is just one part of the P.E.S.R.
formula. Now, we are going to look a little closer at
two other aspects of the routine, Play and Eat. How
do you play with your puppy, and what should he eat?
Let's start with eating and food games in the next
chapter.

Chapter 5
Life Beyond the Bowl

"Every night it's the same ... I have supper in my red dish and drinking water in my yellow dish ... Tonight I think I'll have my supper in the yellow dish and my drinking water in the red dish. Life is too short not to live it up a little!"

Snoopy

If there's one item you won't be using much in the next few months, it's your dog's bowl.

Forget the conventional wisdom saying your dog will eat twice a day, breakfast and dinner, from his bowl. Yours <u>won't</u> be doing that.

Not for a while anyway.

He can still have three or four meals a day, depending on what your breeder has recommended, but he WON'T be eating those meals from a bowl. And here's why …

Food is the secret weapon you are going to use to train, play, bond with and influence your puppy.

This means you need to think carefully about *what* exactly you are going to feed your puppy.

What to feed your puppy?

There's no 100% right answer to this, although completely avoiding bright shiny packets of processed dog food sitting on supermarket shelves would be highly recommended.

Over the years I've fed my dogs everything from table scraps to raw, with lots of kibble variations and wet food in there too.

There's no one perfect food for all dogs.

My Dogue de Bordeaux, Derek, loves raw food, but Sidney's stomach is too sensitive for it, and so he is on a good quality, high-meat-content dry kibble, which we mix in with whatever human leftovers we haven't managed to scoff ourselves earlier that day.

I must stress I'm *not* a nutritionist or a vet, so if you want a more in-depth overview of this then you need to do your own research. You can check out the different kinds of commercial dog food available and what's in them by heading to allaboutdogfood.co.uk

Using the food

When we are talking about your puppy's food, we need to go beyond what the nutritional properties of the food are, and instead think about the practical ways you are going to use it.

Because make no mistake, you are going to 'use the food'.

Food is one of your puppy's most precious resources. Like humans, dogs literally cannot live without it. This means your puppy's food is a high-value resource he will be extremely motivated to get access to. And to channel his inbuilt drive and motivation for food, we need to get creative with how we use it.

Beyond the bowl

Let's take a regular bowl of food that would be hoovered up by most puppies in less than a minute. Your dog gets on average two meals a day, or actually maybe three, four or five meals a day, while he is a young puppy. Well, even if you feed your puppy five meals a day, that's still only five minutes spent eating out of the 1,440 minutes available!

Now, let's look instead at all the different ways you can use that food to play with, train and entertain your puppy.

Trick training with food

If you are feeding kibble then it's likely you will have around 50 small pieces in one serving.

Well, that's 50 individual treats which you can use to reward your dog for doing a trick. And I've got a bunch of tricks coming up in chapter 7 that you and your dog will LOVE learning together.

Each trick you teach is an opportunity for you not only to bond and teach your dog but also to remind him you are a teacher, a provider and a source of good things.

Scent training with food

Food can be used to provide a sensory experience for your puppy. One that will tire him out, keep him focused on a game and make him feel like a superhero. I'm talking about a nose game or scentwork exercise.

Now, don't think your dog needs to enrol in 'police school' to be a scentwork specialist. On the contrary you can provide your dog with some simple nose games by just hiding the odd treat or piece of kibble behind a strategically placed cushion on your living room floor. Get another family member to hold your dog while you show him a treat and then place it behind the cushion. Then let him go find it. Be sure to praise your puppy when he eventually tracks down the treat.

You can also place a trail of five or six pieces of kibble and allow your puppy to follow the trail and be rewarded as he goes. Or how about using treats to get your dog to go to bed? You can lay a trail of treats to lead your puppy, Hansel and Gretel style, all the way into his crate, where inside you could have a tasty KONG waiting, or a small pile of treats for your dog to munch on while you close the door behind him. That's a scentwork session, a training exercise and a food game all rolled into one. Bazinga!

Food games

This leads me nicely onto KONGs. KONGs are tough funny-shaped rubber cones you stuff with your dog's food to make it difficult for him to get out. KONGs and other food-dispensing toys are an absolute godsend for the working pet dog owner.

So why would you want to make it difficult for your dog to eat?

Well, you obviously you don't want to starve your dog, but as I said earlier, your dog's food, if eaten straight from the bowl, will usually disappear in a matter of seconds.

This is less than ideal when you consider your dog's food is one of the most enjoyable parts of his day.

Us humans have books, films, music, television, Netflix, conversations with friends, hobbies and all manner of other things to keep us entertained during the day. Your dog has whatever indoor interactions you are prepared to give him, his daily walk and food. That's about it.

Granted, dogs sleep a large part of the day, and puppies need even more sleep, but it still makes perfect sense to give your dog as many activities as you can to keep him happy and entertained, even when you are not there.

How to entertain your dog with food while you are at work

KONGs can be enjoyed by your dog in his crate, while you are at work. Almost all dogs LOVE eating their daily ration from a food dispenser. They get to lick, sniff, bite and chew the KONGs, which allows them to use their amazingly strong jaws and supersonic scent powers.

The food dispenser turns a fast food meal into an enjoyable challenge that will take your dog a long time to finish.

How long it takes him to finish depends on how well you pack the KONG, but even just spooning the kibble into a KONG and shoving a dog biscuit in the end will provide way more enjoyment for him than just feeding from a bowl.

Using treat dispensers is a crucial part of the **Play, Eat, Sleep, Repeat** formula I talked about in the previous chapter. The key is to have lots of different treat dispensers.

Think of this as an investment in your dog's future happiness.

I suppose your dog could manage with just one KONG (other treat dispensers are available), but then technically I suppose you could manage with just one pair of shoes, but you don't, do you? We all enjoy variety, and a variety of treat dispensers means you can mix up what *and* how you feed your dog, which will add so much enjoyment to his life, and help you prevent unwanted behaviours occurring.

So don't skimp on the treat dispensers and make sure you invest in a few different kinds.

Other ways to use the food

So far we've turned the lowly bowl of dog food into a canine currency you can use to pay your dog when you teach him tricks, or as a smelly scent game reward he can sniff out and enjoy at home or outside, and you transformed a quick meal into a gastronomic challenge in the form of a taste-filled treat dispenser your dog will love removing the food from while *you* are busy at work, or just to help him settle down in his crate.

But that's not all, because your puppy's food is *also* an important training aid you will use to reward him for coming back when you call him (recall training), for walking calmly by your side (not pulling on the lead) and for sitting or lying down when guests arrive at your home (not jumping up).

Of course, all of that will only happen if you heed the main message in this chapter, which is to throw away the bowl (or at least stick it in a kitchen cupboard for a few months).

Your puppy's food routine

The best way to get into a good food routine is to pour your dog's food ration for the day into a large container or Puppaware box (see what I did there ...). Then simply divide it into as many servings as you like, guided by the activities you are going to do with your dog that day.

So if it's a Saturday and you have lots of time to spend with your puppy then you could split it five ways:

- One fifth to be fed by hand, practising tricks.
- Two fifths put in a treat bag (or placed in your coat pocket) to be used to be fed to your puppy on his so-cialisation walks.
- One fifth to be fed from a treat-dispensing toy.

- And one fifth to be used to feed your puppy while you practise grooming and touching him, to get him used to being handled while he's at the vet's.

Bingo!

Then, if it was a Monday and you had to go to work and leave your puppy for longer periods of time, you might want to up the amount he eats from a treat dispenser to two or even three fifths.

I don't want to be too prescriptive because only you know your own individual routine, but I will say please ensure you make full use of this most precious and finite resource.

For more cool and useful ideas on the best ways to use your dog's food, I would highly recommend you invest in book 3 in the Street-Smart Dog Training series, *The Hungry Games*. Available from;

www.mydogssuperhero.com/thehungrygames

How to use the food to teach your dog English

One of the most important things you will teach your puppy in the first few months of his life is human hands are kind, loving, affectionate and he has nothing to fear from them.

And you do this by simply feeding him by hand. For this to happen consistently you need to have the food nearby. I always have a little bowl of my dog's treats or kibble on the mantelpiece, out of his reach. That way I can reward my puppy when he randomly does something good, and I can also squeeze in a three-minute impromptu training session when the Coronation Street ad break is happening …

Your puppy's first life lesson

We will be starting a trick training programme in the following chapter, but one trick you can start straight away is to teach your puppy his name.

I like my puppies to know they should come to me when they hear their name, because good things are going to happen.

So I teach my puppy his name by rewarding him every time he looks at me and comes towards me when I say his name.

You can do this on your own by sitting on the floor with a handful of your dog's kibble.

Show him the kibble and give him a couple of pieces. Then show him a piece and place it gently an arm's length away from you. Let him go and get it. He will eat it and then head back to you for some more. As he heads back towards you, you can say his name in a nice cheery voice.

Repeat this several times and mix up the rewards so sometimes you just stroke, smile and speak to him and other times you give him a piece of kibble.

The other way to do this is to have one family member hold the puppy while the other one goes to the other end of the room and waves a toy at him. Then the 'holder' places the puppy on the floor and the 'toy waver' calls the puppy's name. You can get some great running recalls going between family members, and your puppy will soon learn that his name means come here because fun things will happen.

Training handling skills

One huge mistake we made with our first dog, Flo, was not getting her used to being handled by humans. She was a nine-week-old rat bag when we rescued her from the kennels, and she remained much the same for the next 14 years. That's not strictly true as she became, in my eyes, the model dog for the last six years of her life.

But her early weeks had obviously been quite stressful and unsettled, and because of that she was quite a wild and feral puppy.

That's only one side of the story though, and I represented the other half of the equation. And I made the most fatal of errors which many new puppy owners make ... I got a dog when I knew diddly-squat about dogs!

Flo was a terror, and *I* was an idiot. Not a great combination.

My wife had grown up with Staffies her whole life, but Flo was a challenge even for her.

We struggled through the entire puppyhood phase, and this wasn't made any easier by the fact we actually acquired the dog two weeks after we moved into our first home, with a six-month-old baby in tow.

Like I said, not a good recipe for success.

The sad thing is I know I could have drastically improved Flo's behaviour and moulded her into a much easier-to-manage dog if I'd known the contents of this chapter.

Hindsight is a wonderful thing, and there are lots of things I would have done differently if I could have my time with her again. At the top of the list of things would be to teach her to not be afraid of being handled and touched. But because I didn't teach my dog handling skills I ended up enduring miserable vet's visits for Flo's entire life.

She simply hated being touched anywhere on her body. Bandaging a cut paw of hers was a test of strength and endurance, and even just a regular vet's check-up would mean I had to clamp my hands around her jaws and hold her still while the vet checked her over.

It upsets me to think about this, let alone write about it, but when the time came for Flo to be put to sleep at the vet's, despite being old, weak and slightly delirious because of the epilepsy she was suffering from, I still had to hold her down firmly while the vet administered the drug that would sadly end her life.

Losing a dog is never a nice moment, but those final minutes with Flo could have been made more memorable if she hadn't disliked being handled by anyone, including me.

That's what I want you to avoid, and you can easily achieve that, and have a dog who is not only happy to be handled but positively enjoys it by following the 'handling plan' coming up next.

For this exercise you will need:

- your dog's collar and lead
- a bowl of kibble, with maybe some treats mixed in too
- a dog brush.

I like to do this exercise with my puppy on a table, although you can do it sitting, kneeling or even lying down with your puppy.

I like to use a table because the puppy is less likely (though not entirely less likely) to move off the table.

Also, and this is the big reason, getting your puppy used to standing still and being handled on a table is the exact same setup he will face in the groomer's and the vet's.

Training your puppy to be good at the vet's

Place a large cloth on the table and attach your puppy's lead to his collar. Lift your puppy on the table then hold the lead in one hand and keep it quite short.

Then place the treat bowl nearby and start grooming your puppy.

I would recommend you teach your puppy to tolerate being groomed with a brush even if he isn't a breed who needs any grooming. At some point in your puppy's life, you are going to have to inspect his hair for ticks, mites, chewing gum (yes, it happens) and to locate the piece of fox shit he rolled in earlier in the day which is now making your puppy smell like he crawled out of a coffin. Well, all that is much easier to do *if* you get your puppy used to being handled and touched in all his nooks and crannies, now.

- Start with a brush or just running your hand down your puppy's back, then progress to going along the back and down one of his back legs.
- Next you can stroke your puppy from his head and then down his shoulder and down his front leg.
- As your puppy gets used to being handled you can progress to softly gripping your puppy as you stroke him, kind of a light massage grip, not forgetting to talk to your puppy all the time and tell him how clever he is.

Next we move onto what your puppy might feel is rather invasive handling. This is where the treats come in.

- Have your bowl of kibble nearby (not in front of your puppy where he can see it or he WILL eat it), and once again run your hand slowly down your puppy's back, and down by his thigh, past his knee and down to his paw. Then pick the paw up and give it a nice gentle rub. Then pop his foot back down and say "Good boy" and give him a piece of food.
- Repeat this with <u>all four paws</u>.
- You should repeat the whole exercise with each paw, only this time when you hold the paw you are going to count to three before you place it down and reward your puppy. Make sure you are smiling and praising your puppy all the time.
- Gradually increasing the handling time like this is going to gradually increase your puppy's tolerance for being handled.

That would be a good place to stop for a break. When I've finished any training or a handling session I like to play a little game with my puppy to reward him for being so good. He will eventually associate the game with the handling and training, and so playing helps your puppy see the handling exercise as an enjoyable activity.

After a break, or even the next day, you can repeat this exercise, and in stages move onto your puppy's ears, eyes, mouth and bum.

Yep, you read that right. I said bum. Don't worry; you aren't going fully internal, but it's good to get your puppy used to being touched and handled everywhere. You never know what illness will require him to be handled by a vet. At some point your vet is going to check your dog's temperature with a thermometer up his bum, so get your dog used to this by touching around the bum area (obviously without actually putting anything up his bum).

Training your puppy to enjoy having his ears touched

That sounds like an oxymoron. I mean, surely no one in their right mind would enjoy having their ears touched? I know I certainly don't.

However, I'm a human who can be reasoned with, and when I have an ear infection, I put my fears to one side and I'm a big brave boy while the doctor checks my lugs (and if I'm really good I get a lollipop for my troubles).

Your dog, however, can't be reasoned with in the same way. You can't sit your dog down and say *"Look, fella, I know you don't approve of anyone raking around your ear, but you have a seed stuck in there which will get infected if we don't remove it, so be a good chap and sit still while we do the necessary"*.

Your dog will twist his head and make it impossible for the vet to do his job, unless … you've got him used to having his ears and eyes checked while he was a puppy, so …

- Start by just massaging your puppy's head and whole ear; then progress to holding the ear flap between your finger and thumb and gently massage, rewarding with kibble now and again. If your puppy likes tummy rubs (and who doesn't?) then you can gently inspect your puppy's ear with one hand while rubbing his tummy with the other.
- Then, if your puppy is managing well enough, you can progress to the inside of the ear. Use a clean cloth and gently wipe the inside of the ear in a circular motion. Finger in, wipe, finger out, then a nice reward and cuddle. Well done, dog!

As you did before with the paws you want to gradually increase the amount of time you can have your finger inside your dog's ear. Work up to 10 seconds, although this may take a few weeks to achieve by practising just a few minutes each day.

Easy eye checks

You can repeat the same routine with the eyes, as you did with the ears. Start by holding your puppy's head still for a second, as you look into his eyes. Gradually increase the time you hold him. Then you can get him used to having his eyes wiped by using a clean, damp paper towel or tissue.

All of my dogs have needed eye or ear drops sometime in their lives. Yours probably will too, and completing these short regular ear and eye check-ups now is going to make administering future medicines a cake-walk.

Manageable mouth examination

Finally we have the mouth area. This is one place you will struggle to get immediate access to. You can make it much more likely your puppy will open his mouth by gently holding the top and bottom of his jaw with each of your hands, and then as soon as you have the mouth open simply pop a piece of chicken or another tasty treat in there.

This will at least get him used to readily opening his mouth.

Then you can start rubbing just your finger across your puppy's gums. As before, use the treats to reward him and gradually build up your puppy's tolerance for having his gums massaged.

Then you can add a small quantity of doggy toothpaste to your finger and make sure your puppy is comfortable before you move onto using a doggy toothbrush.

Doggy dentist

Doggy dental treatment can be expensive, so cleaning your dog's teeth once a month like this can potentially save you a fortune. Although the diet your dog is on also plays a big part in how his teeth turn out.

My Dogue de Bordeaux, Derek, is on a raw diet, and so because of the bones and lack of additives has pearly-white gnashers, while Sid has been on more dry food and consequently has more plaque on his teeth, which I have to remove using the method described above.

So that's the handling routine. Do this regularly and your puppy will actually enjoy going to the vet's and being handled.

Handling health check

This kind of handling session also acts as a great health check for your puppy. You will be able to keep a much better handle on his weight and any little injuries he picks up, *if* you regularly (weekly would work) do a handling session like this.

One of my previous clients owned a giant schnauzer who hated being groomed so much he actually had a heart attack. When she got the next dog I made sure he was more than happy to be groomed. We had regular visits to the groomer's BEFORE he was even groomed just to meet them and get him used to standing on the table. And I did a lot of work at home, using the handling techniques I have shown you, which I then built on by using scissors (clipped slightly away from the dog), electric razors and hairdryers (which I used to massage the dog with) to get him used to the feeling of being groomed and dried.

If your puppy is going to require regular grooming then I suggest you follow a similar routine.

How to use food to make your dog love you

Finally, another thing you can do with food, just as you can with play and affection, is reward your puppy for doing spontaneously good things.

In the trick training chapter to come I show you how to lure your dog into a sit, or a down, but you can also reward and encourage your puppy to do what you want by 'capturing' his good behaviour.

So if your puppy decides to run towards you when you bend over to tie your shoelace, then reward him with praise, affection and even a treat. If you capture this behaviour often enough then he will naturally start running towards you whenever you lower yourself onto your haunches.

Rewarding eye contact

Eye contact should also be rewarded regularly and with great enthusiasm by you. Personally, I want my dogs to think that looking at me is something worthwhile doing regularly, so I reward all eye contact with my dog. Not often with treats actually, but always with a smile and a stroke of the head, and a "Good boy".

Capturing behaviours like this makes it more likely your dog will look at you or 'check in' with you when he is off lead at the park too.

Summary

- Food is fuel for your puppy, and a good diet is essential for his physical development. Exactly how you use food will play a big part in how easy your puppy is to manage. Using the food correctly means NOT wasting it by feeding from a bowl. Be sure to invest in lots of treat-dispensing toys to entertain your dog and feed him at the same time.

- Handling skills – Having a puppy who is happy to go to the vet's and groomer's is a dream, and alternatively owning a dog who hates being touched, handled or groomed is a total nightmare; even simple jobs like checking his ears or removing thorns from his feet can be fraught with danger. Make sure you do some grooming, handling and a general daily health check with your new puppy.

- Many a time I've been in the park and watched in horror as an owner repeatedly screams their dog's name in vain as he completely ignores them and continues arsing around. I feel like asking "Are you sure that's your dog's name?" but I don't. I'm nice like that. It does stress how important it is to teach your puppy his name, and when you say it he should come to you because good things happen. Doing this consistently now will set you up to have a dog who recalls anywhere you let him off lead.

BONUS – To help you further master 'using the food' I've put together a Puppy Food Games Masterclass which will more clearly demonstrate a lot of the activities laid out in this chapter. To access this FREE masterclass go to:

www.mydogssuperhero.com/perfectpuppyproject

The Perfect Puppy Project

Chapter 6

How to Teach Your Puppy to Love You
(and always want to be with you!)

"The devotion of dogs has been greatly exaggerated. What a dog really wants is excitement. He is easily bored, cannot amuse himself, and therefore demands entertainment. The dog's ideal life is a life of active uselessness."
William Lyon Phelps

I was born, raised and still live in Sunderland, a seaside city which sits on the coast in the North East of England.

Sunderland used to be dominated by two thriving industries, the shipyards and the mines, which provided the main employment in the town. Until the 1970s most men would leave school at 16 with two career choices, and end up going either to the shipyards or down the pit.

My dad went down the pit aged 19, as did my grandad and my great-grandad. Who knows where I would be if the mines hadn't closed in the mid-1980s ...

My grandad and great-grandad were traditional miners who worked on the coal face, but my dad was an electrician, and like all the other electricians, welders, joiners and fitters he served an apprenticeship when he first start working there.

The system of apprenticeships was first developed in the late Middle Ages. A master craftsman was entitled to employ young people as an inexpensive form of labour, in exchange for providing food, lodging and formal training in the craft.

In many jobs such as construction, engineering and catering, this practical, on-the-job learning is the only way to master the necessary skills and is essential if you want to be able to complete the tasks in the real world and not just in a classroom.

This practical approach very much applies to dog training, especially if you want your puppy to have real-world experiences and be as well behaved off lead in the park as he is at home.

You must recognise that as your dog's owner, you are his keeper, his best friend AND his teacher.

This means you need to rethink what dog training is and understand that dog training is *not* just something you do when your dog starts developing bad habits.

Dog training is an activity you need to do all the time if you want to prevent bad behaviours developing. And by continually training and developing your little apprentice you will gradually mould your puppy into the kind of dog you want him to be.

Real-world training

As an example of real-world training versus theory-based training, think about a dog who has been taught to do a brilliant 30-second stay from 10 yards away in a church hall training class but is unable to give his owner eye contact in a busy park because he's too easily distracted.

Or the dog who is amazing at flyball but is completely uncontrollable when off leash at the beach.

Or the dog who has passed his Kennel Club Good Citizen Dog Scheme Award, but who can't be left home alone because he destroys the furniture and howls and disturbs the neighbours.

I'm not in any way knocking training classes here because there are many activities you could try with your dog in the future.

But first and foremost, you need to develop a solid bond with your puppy, so he enjoys being with you. This means not allowing him to do anything as a puppy you don't want him to do as an adult dog.

And it means putting effort into your interactions with your puppy so he sees you as the keeper of the keys to the 'fun zone'.

That is exactly what you are going to learn to do in the 'puppy apprenticeship' I have all laid out, over the next two chapters.

A human apprenticeship can last from one to four years, but I have put together a plan of action to enable to you to manage, bond with, train and have lots of fun with your puppy over these tricky first few months together.

First we are going to look at how to play and interact with your puppy; then in the next chapter I'm going to show you some simple tricks you can teach him.

Toy Story

I'm assuming you've bought some toys for your puppy, and if you haven't then you need to rectify that now by investing in some, or making your own from old socks, gloves and tea towels. This is a perfectly acceptable option. Your dog won't turn up his nose like a socially anxious teenager because the toys you expect him to play with don't have designer labels on them.

In fact, my dog training mentor and good friend David Davies showed me exactly how special non-traditional dog toys could be on our first training session together.

It's not about the toy but what you do with it that matters

I arrived at Dave's house with my dog Derek and a bag full of shiny new dog toys in tow. No expense spared for my Derek. Then Dave came out with a scruffy old haversack filled with what can only be described as junk. I looked on bemused as he tried to play with Derek using old gloves and short lengths of hosepipe, but Dave had the last laugh when Derek started jumping around because he wanted the 'pretend' toys.

An important lesson learned by me, and it's one you need to take on board as we enter this chapter, which is all about playing with your puppy.

Remember, it's not the toy, it's what YOU do with it that matters ...

Whether you use homemade or shop-bought toys is by the by; what matters is you have some because toys are an important weapon in your dog training armoury.

You are going use them often, to play and bond with your puppy.

Dogs of any age can be playful creatures, but puppies take playing to a whole new level. Your puppy WILL want to play. You need to teach him *what* to play with, and *where* he can put his teeth while he is playing; that's if you want to avoid the sore fingers and scratched arms that come with unwanted biting and chewing.

Why do puppies bite?

Your puppy has grown up in an environment where he regularly rough and tumbled with his brothers and sisters. During these games he also used his teeth a lot and was probably disciplined by his mum with her teeth when he was playing too roughly.

You are obviously not going to bite your puppy. That would be stupid. Nor are you going to roughly handle, pin to the floor, shush, snarl or hit your puppy. That would also be pretty silly, unproductive and cruel. Even 'dog whisperer' style 'touching' a.k.a. punching your dog is not recommended. Just because someone is on TV doing something *doesn't* mean to say you should try to copy.

Confession time

Once upon a time, before I started my dog training journey, I too used to watch the *Dog Whisperer* show. I marvelled at his magical ability to control a pack of dogs with his sheer presence. So I bought the books, and the T-shirt, and copied what I saw, and the harsh and unnecessary training methods made me and my dogs miserable.

Don't make the mistake I did, and please ensure any training you do, or you are taught to do, is fair and effective.

Back to puppy biting …

There are two schools of thought when it comes to puppy biting. One school says puppies need to learn 'bite inhibition'. This means the puppy needs to learn how hard he can bite the human, or to bite the human 'gently'.

The second school teaches that puppies (and dogs) should learn they can't touch the humans' skin or clothes with their teeth. Both of these methods can work, but I am going to teach you method number two, which is to teach your puppy *not* to touch human skin with his teeth.

This is the method I personally use, and I think it's the easiest and safest way to quickly teach your puppy not to put his teeth on any human skin.

Mouthy mutts

There's a good reason you should teach your puppy to have a nice soft mouth, because mouthy dogs, i.e. dogs who regularly mouth their owner's hands, are incredibly annoying, not to mention painful.

You'll feel mortified when your puppy is mouthing guests who come to visit. You will likely tell him off, which in turn will make your puppy think people don't like him.

The solution is to knock that behaviour on the head by following this simple training plan.

This chapter is essentially about playing with your dog, but I'm going to teach you this bite prevention plan first, so when you start playing with your puppy, and he gets too excited, and he WILL get too excited at some point, then you know exactly what you need to do to, pardon the pun, to 'nip' the biting behaviour in the bud.

How to stop your puppy biting

At some point while you are playing with your puppy he is going to accidentally overreach with his mouth, and instead of grabbing the toy or the food, he is going to bite you. He may even bite when he jumps up at you when you walk in a room.

Now, the chances are you *will* feel his pin-like teeth, but it won't actually hurt you, and it certainly shouldn't break your skin.

However, that's not what your puppy will think …

The Perfect Puppy Project

As soon as your puppy's teeth touch your skin I want you to recoil and say *"OW!"* in a high-pitched voice. Furrow your brow, look at where his teeth touch your hand and rub it profusely saying *"Oh, that really hurts, Mammy is in a lot of pain, why would my lovely new puppy do such a thing?"*

I'm looking for an Oscar-winning performance from you here, so don't let me down. Your puppy should be under the illusion he has hurt you.

Then you can resume the game, or whatever it is you were doing with him. The next time your puppy's teeth touch your hand, I want you to repeat the whole *"Ow, ouch, that really hurt!"* piece, only this time you are also going to immediately take your puppy to his 'time out' place, which needs to be nearby, but out of the room, i.e. away from you.

It's a simple three-step routine.

1. The puppy bites (either on purpose, or by mistake).
2. Then you cry foul (or ouch!).
3. Then you immediately take him for a one-minute 'time out'.

The time out is the puppy's consequence for biting. This is why you don't need to scold or hit the puppy. Simply removing him from the room will do the trick.

If you have followed this programme closely so far, and spent lots of time bonding and playing with him, then your puppy should think the sun shines out of your arse, and he will be truly gutted when a game ends abruptly, and he is removed from the room.

Key points to remember

The time out should only last one minute. So for one minute your puppy is in the kitchen, or the hall, or in a small room with a baby gate on it. And it doesn't matter if he whines, barks or scratches at the door, you are going to ignore him.

Then once the minute is up, you can open the door and allow your puppy to enter the room. It's important here you don't fawn all over your puppy and feel sorry for him. You negate the effectiveness of the training if you act like his best friend straight away. That's like a parent telling a child off for stealing, then seeing the child upset reward them with a present. It's not consistent and confusing for the child.

So when he slinks back in the room, be a little cool with him for a further minute and then resume the activity.

After five or six 'time outs' (sometimes less) most puppies get the idea biting is bad, and many never bite again. It will likely take a few days or maybe a week for him to really get the message, but if everyone in the house is consistent then he will learn much faster.

Speed is of the essence

The final point to note is you must be quick with your reaction and when you deliver the punishment, i.e. when you remove him from the room.

So as soon as he bites you need to say *"OW!"* and then pick him up and get him out a few seconds later.

It's no good continuing your conversation with a friend, or finishing off a text message, and *then* taking the puppy out. If you want him to figure out he's being punished for biting, then you need to remove him from the room <u>as soon as he bites you</u>.

How to teach a soft mouth

You can further encourage a nice soft mouth by feeding your puppy by hand. So take small piece of his kibble and hold it between your finger and thumb and show it to your puppy.

He will sniff it, lick it and eventually try to take the piece of kibble from you. He can indeed take it, but *only* when his teeth are touching the kibble. Teeth on skin or fingers means no treat, and any harsh biting needs to be dealt with using the same method as before.

Just as he did when playing with toys, your puppy will learn he isn't allowed to put teeth on skin, even when there are things around he likes.

So now you have a strategy for what to do when your puppy plays too roughly, next I should show you how to actually play with him …

Playing with toys

Toy exercise:

Choose one of your puppy's toys, something raggy or snakelike will be good.

Get on the floor with the toy and get his attention with it. By get his attention, I don't mean shove it in his face and say "LOOK HERE, IS FUN, PLAY NOW, PUPPY!" No, we are going to be a bit subtler than that.

We know dogs almost always want stuff other people have, so if your puppy isn't immediately interested in you, then you can tease him just a little.

In a nice cheery voice, you can say something like *"Oooh, what's this I've got? Isn't this the most interesting and best toy ever?"* Then try to tempt your puppy towards you with it.

Don't get disheartened if he doesn't jump up straight away; you will have to put in a bit of effort and encourage him. Try to get a bit of interaction going with the toy, but don't be tempted to just give it to him. The idea is you are teaching him to like *you*, and like doing stuff *with you* because you have stuff *he* likes.

Over the next few days you will start to see your puppy has certain toys he likes more than others. I need you to pay particular attention to what becomes his absolute favourite toy; I call these the 'Kryptonite' and they are going to be extremely helpful when you start taking your puppy to the park.

So once you have your puppy's attention with the toy you are holding, let him have a sniff of it, let him bite or lick it, talk to him and make him feel special.

The game of two toys

The basic premise of two toys is you have two toys (or two hairbrushes or plastic bottles, or whatever safe toy it is your puppy *loves* playing with).

The Perfect Puppy Project

The toys should be almost identical otherwise your puppy will prefer one over the other. First get him interested in one of the toys; then throw or drop the toy a short distance away. When he goes off to see what you have thrown, take out the second toy and start getting him interested.

Dogs usually want what someone else has got, so you can make your toy seem more interesting by using your voice and the way you act. Say your dog's name in a nice cheery voice. Move away from him with it slightly and he may follow; then keep talking to your toy, throw it up and catch it, and make stupid noises, *"Whoop whoop!"*

The moment your puppy drops the first toy, you can drop or throw the one *you* are holding, and then you pick up the first one and start the process again.

Try to drop the second toy on the other side of where you dropped the first. If you make yourself the centre of the game with toys being dropped either side of where you are standing, you will be able to retrieve the dropped toys and control the game better.

This is quite a high-energy game, and puppies really love it. It's crucial you don't try to take the toy from your puppy, but rather wait for him to drop it. That way he learns when he drops a toy he actually gets another one, so this game is going to teach him he doesn't need to run off with things, and it's better to share them with you.

You should be talking to your dog and praising him the whole time, especially when he drops the toy and comes towards you for the toy you are holding.

If you are really struggling to get your dog to drop the first toy you can exchange a little piece of kibble, but it's better to wait it out until he drops it of his own choosing.

The second game is tuggy tugg tugg.

Tuggy tugg tugg

Tuggy is a great game all dogs can play. Some guarding and terrier breeds love playing tuggy more than any other game. But you need to be very careful that you are gentle when playing tuggy with your puppy. If you are too vigorous, you can easily pull his milk teeth out. Also, when you are playing tuggy, try to use a forward-and-back motion rather than side to side, as playing tuggy with a side-to-side action can mimic a killing action for a dog.

You can play tuggy with any item you and your dog can safely hold, but it's easier if it's a cloth or rope-type material. An old towel or tea towel cut into one- to two-foot-long strips with a knot at each end does the job perfectly. I have never met a dog yet who refused to play a game with me because I wasn't using a branded dog toy …

So first get the toy and make it 'come alive', much the same as you did for the other game, only this time you are going to encourage your dog to get hold of it. Don't try to force the toy on him, or he will likely back away from you. You can throw it a short distance or run with it or make it move around the floor and encourage your dog to 'get it'.

You should be telling your dog he is a 'good boy' every time he looks interested or moves towards the toy and also if he attempts to mouth it.

When he does finally hold the toy, tell him he is a 'good boy' and have a short game of tuggy. You need to judge this as you play, but don't be too physical at first, and when your dog gets into it, just stop moving the toy. Keep your arm still and wait for him to let go. And wait and wait. You may have to put two hands on the toy (one on either end of the toy with your dog's mouth gripping the middle). Then, and this is the important bit, when he does let go, praise him with a cheery voice and tell him he's a 'good boy'! And give him his end of the toy straight back again and have another short game of tuggy. Continue this five or six times and then stop. Go and make yourself a brew as a reward and have a sit-down and think about what you did. Your dog can enjoy a biscuit at the same time.

Remember the idea is you are teaching the dog that it's more fun to play with you than it is to keep, run off with and chew up the toy. So you need to teach him the game does not end when the pulling and letting go stops, and it will start back up again. Obviously the game has to end sometime, and when it does, you can just tell your dog he is a 'very good boy' and give him some affection. Leaving him wanting more isn't a bad thing.

You should play this game little and often, and always remember to put the toy away when you are finished playing. Don't fall into the trap of telling your dog to 'LEAVE IT' every two seconds, much better to just wait until he lets go. If you really struggle to get him to leave it, exchange a treat for the toy and then resume the game.

And that's tuggy tugg tugg. It's a great physical game, which most dogs really love. Unlike a retrieving game, it keeps your dog near you all the time, and for dogs that really enjoy playing, it can be a great high-energy reward for doing something they like.

So this has been a busy old chapter. You've learned how to play some simple games with toys, and you know what to do if your puppy bites you, either accidentally or on purpose. These games are going to help you take the edge off your puppy and build a great bond with him; it's also what you will be doing with him during the 'Play' section of the Play, Eat, Sleep, Repeat formula.

But most puppies don't need any encouraging to play; if anything they can be too exuberant. So once we have their attention and focus then it's a good idea to introduce some more formal purposeful puppy training.

That's where trick training comes in during the next chapter.

Summary

- Find the Kryptonite – Spend some time playing and messing around with your puppy on the floor using the toys you have bought or made. Don't overlook the power of a homemade toy. I've seen dogs turn their nose up at expensive shop-bought toys but go crazy when you knot four odd socks together to use as a tug toy. Playing with your puppy will help build his confidence in you so you build a brilliant bond based on trust and fun.

- Puppy biting – All puppies bite, it's natural for them to do so, but they should be taught very quickly that biting humans, even by mistake, has consequences. The consequence in this case is going to be removing the puppy from the room. That might not seem like a big deal to you, but to your puppy it will not be pleasant. To him you are everything, or at least you will be if you play with him regularly as I've laid out in this chapter.

- Almost all dogs can learn to enjoy playing retrieve, find it or tuggy games. Working and gun dog puppies will usually fall in love with those games very quickly. When you spend time playing with your puppy you are effectively teaching him you are a cool person to be with. These games you play and perfect now will be what keep you and your puppy glued together when you begin to exercise him outdoors at the park, beach and woods.

Chapter 7

How to Master the Magnificent Seven Puppy Tricks

"Rambunctious, rumbustious, delinquent dogs become angelic when sitting."

Dr Ian Dunbar

One trick you might be surprised I don't recommend you teach your puppy is a 'paw' or 'high five'. There's nothing wrong with this trick per se; I just find once a dog has been taught to paw, it tends to become his default trick when he wants anything from you.

So if he needs the loo, he gives you his paw.

If he wants a treat or a drink then he gives you a paw.

And if you don't act quick enough he will start giving a paw more forcefully, which essentially means the dog ends up hitting the owner to get what he wants.

When he's nine weeks old this isn't a problem, but fast forward a month or two and it's a different story. The problem is exacerbated when the dog is a large to giant breed, or if you have small children in the house who are more sensitive to being whacked on the leg by a puppy.

So no paw will be taught here, booooo …

But I do have seven magnificent tricks to share with you that are fun and purposeful. Yay!

Yep, there's the 'P' word again. In case you had forgotten we're on a mission now, to turn your playful pup into a delightful dog, and the practical and easy tricks I am going to share with you in this chapter will provide the primary home-schooling education your puppy needs.

First, let's clarify a few things.

By teaching him some tricks at this early age you *aren't* trying to turn your new addition into some kind of puppy prodigy who will be competing on the next episode of *Britain's Got Talent* (although you never know *what* will happen *if* you catch the training bug …).

No, training your puppy with some cool tricks is simply a great way for you to start teaching him what is expected of him, and what he has to do to reach the venerable status all dogs aspire to, i.e. how to be a *'good boy'*!

Trick training will also help you learn about your puppy's body language, and even more important for him, it will begin the process of teaching him about human body language.

And all the while you are training your puppy, you are constantly reminding and reinforcing to him good things (toys, treats and affection) come from you.

This is how you make your puppy love (and want to be with) YOU.

Your puppy prodigy

Your puppy is a sponge who is capable of learning new things very fast. Trick training is going to engage your puppy's mind, and tire him out mentally, so he sleeps and settles more quickly.

This is an essential part of the Play, Eat, Sleep, Repeat routine.

Regular trick training sessions also help add structure to your puppy's day and give you something to do with him instead of just cuddling …

Cuddles are awesome but any lazy moron can sit and cuddle a dog all day, and many lazy morons do just that. It takes consistency and a commitment to training to have a really great dog, and teaching him to perform some tricks is going to be fun for you, your family *and* your puppy; not to mention tricks are an awesome way to show off how clever your puppy is when guests arrive.

When to start trick training

You can start trick training the second you bring your puppy home; just remember he will be tired from the journey, and the excitement of meeting your family, and even if he isn't he will soon tire once he's got acclimatised to his new home.

But even on the first day, once he's rested a while, you can begin teaching him a couple of tricks, and we are going to start with the classic 'sit' and then a 'down'.

'Sit' is an incredibly useful trick that gives your puppy something to do instead of jumping up at you, or anyone else.

Trick training

There are many ways to teach tricks to your puppy, but as usual, I'm going to show you the easiest way to do it, using a technique called luring.

Learning through luring

Luring is all about showing your dog what you want him to do. Think of it as using something like a ball or food to guide your dog into whatever position you want him in.

And I'm going to borrow the name of one of my first dog training clients (a female German pointer) called Aster to help you remember how to teach your dog anything using the luring method.

But first we need to lose the 'e' from her name so we are left with ASTR, which stands for:

A – Attention

S – Show

T – Tell

R – Reward

Let's use teaching a 'sit' as an example, so I can explain how my ASTR method works.

You will need:

- a toy or treat
- your dog
- some enthusiasm.

'Sit'

First make sure your puppy has seen the toy or treat by putting it in front of his face (or nose for food). This is the first stage in the trick training process, you getting your dog's ATTENTION.

Slowly move your hand holding the treat from his nose to just above his head. Then wait for him to put his bum on the floor. If he doesn't, just take it back to his nose again, and move it even more slowly above his head. Maybe change the angle this time, so you are going more above his head then back towards his neck (slowly) or above his head towards you. Take your time with this and be patient. Your puppy doesn't know what you want him to do, but he will do very soon, and once he's got it, he will easily do it all. This is you SHOWING your dog what you want him to do.

Once your puppy has done it a few times, you can TELL him the command. So once he starts sitting regularly, you should then say "Sit". Your dog doesn't speak English, and it's much easier to pair the command to the action than it is to repeat '"Sit" 17 times while you wait for your dog to sit.

As soon as your dog's bum hits the floor, you say "Good boy" and give him his REWARD (a game of tug or a little piece of kibble). Repeat this and once your dog has done it four or five times and has the idea, *then* you can start to add the 'sit' command as his bum hits the floor. That's your 'tell', so you tell him what you want. Repeat another four or five times until he is sitting as you say "Sit".

Phasing out the treats

Once your dog has the hang of it and is regularly following the command, try to lure him into position using just your hand. Place the piece of kibble on a bench or in your pocket. Then when he sits, get the food out, make a huge fuss and give him a small piece of food.

You should repeat this until you think your dog is doing the action when you say the command almost every time; then put the toys and treats to one side and have a little break.

In the break you should put the kettle on and tell your dog how bloody clever you think he is, and give him some affection. I want you to go overboard with the affection and the praise. Your puppy will enjoy it, and he will associate the whole training session with having a good time with you. Using lots of praise and affection will mean you are not completely dependent on the toys and treats to keep your dog's focus on you. You will enjoy it too.

So there you go; that's how to teach a 'sit' using luring, and you have ASTR to help you remember which order to go in.

It's not hard at all, is it?

No, Dom, it isn't.

Don't forget you need to have your puppy's attention before you start training a trick, so you should always play with him a little before you start. Think of this as a warm-up.

Training tips:

Be careful you don't use too high a value item of food when you begin your training indoors. There are a couple of reasons for this.

Using a treat that is too tasty or a toy which is too stimulating is going to have your dog jumping at you to get at it. You want to use something he wants, but won't go mental for, so his regular dry kibble will do just fine for now.

The other reason is you will need to use the higher-value items when you take the training outside, and there are more distractions around. Also, it just makes more sense to train this way.

If you were starting a new job, and on the first day at work you got a big fat bonus and a new car as soon as you walked in, then you would probably struggle to motivate yourself on days two, three and four.

So let's think long term and make your puppy work a little even for a low-value treat. Of course, you are going to use your voice and affection so that even the low-value food feels more rewarding for your dog.

So where do we go now? Well, if you really want to progress with your training, you should do two things.

1) Start teaching another trick. I would recommend a 'down' then 'spin' followed by 'catch it' and then 'through the legs'. I have instructions for you to follow so you can teach each new trick using the same luring technique, just as you did with the 'sit'.

2) But just as important as starting something new is to lock down the trick you have just taught. So start practising your 'sit' in the kitchen and other rooms in the house, BEFORE you do the same thing in the garden, the street and eventually the park. Don't expect your puppy to sit automatically straight away in another room on command, but each time you practise a trick your puppy should pick it up a little quicker in each new room you practise in.

Make it easy for yourself and always have some food to hand. You probably won't need to do as much luring as you did in the sitting room, or if you do, you will more quickly be able to start luring with just your hand, but be prepared to use some toys or treats to get him going. One thing you absolutely must do is talk to your puppy; say his name, and use praise and affection before, during and after whenever you practise anything. Then he will have fun and enjoy it, and he will want to do it again.

The second point is critical, as this whole trick section is the start of you building a routine of things to do with your puppy on a daily basis, wherever you take him. You will have a whole routine of activities which he loves doing with you, but we start this training indoors where it's easiest to learn. Then by the time your puppy is ready to go for walks to the park, you will have already built an amazing bond with him, which will help you deal with distractions and keep him glued to your side.

Teaching other tricks:

'Down'

You can lure your puppy to a 'down' from a 'sit' or a 'stand'. I will describe it from a 'sit' as that's the exercise we have just done, but feel free to go from a 'stand' or whatever is easier for you.

So think ASTR, and first get your Kryptonite and get your puppy's attention.

From a 'sit' position, move your hand from your puppy's face area (to make sure he has seen the toy or smelt the food) and slowly move your hand down towards the floor in front of him. You can encourage him to get it or follow it down to the floor. But don't say "Down" yet, remember. We are at the 'SHOW' part, where we show him what we want him to do.

You may have more success moving the toy slowly down between your dog's front paws, and he should slowly slide down into the 'down' position. Again, this isn't a race, so take your time with it.

Dogs are a bit like humans in that some are cleverer and quicker than others, and from experience I can tell you my cocker spaniel, Sid, learned to do a 'sit', 'down', 'spin' and 'rollover' in the same time it took me to get some eye contact from Barry the Bordeaux. Remember this isn't a competition, and you should challenge and push your dog, but go at a pace to suits him, and always make sure it's fun for him. On that subject, with all these exercises and tricks, always reward your puppy for trying, so if he even attempts a 'down' and slides down just a little, you should tell him he's a 'good boy'.

Encouragement is the key here. We want him to enjoy it and want to do it again, so make it pleasurable. You should never get to a point where you feel frustrated with your puppy. Be patient and if you think he's struggling with any of the tricks, then have time out, remind yourself it's not your puppy's fault and have another go later on.

Training tip:

Some dogs just aren't keen on doing a 'down', so don't stress if your puppy doesn't fancy it, or maybe try on a different floor surface. If your dog keeps moving backwards, you could try the exercise with your dog's back end facing a wall or your couch. Then as you go from a 'sit' to a 'down', he can't back away from you. This sometimes helps them into a 'down' position. Then as soon as your dog gets near a 'down' position, you can tell him he is a 'good boy' and give him some affection or a little piece of food. Repeat this, keeping it light and fun. Start getting into a rhythm of practising something five or six times and then having a little break. When your dog is going into a 'down' regularly, you can start to add the 'TELL' ('down') command as his chest hits the floor. Again, repeat five or six times.

There is a slightly quicker and more direct way to teach this to dogs that are particularly toy or food motivated.

Get down on your haunches with your dog, and make the toy or food 'come alive' to get his attention, and then move your hand from side to side across your dog's face so your dog is following your hand intently and looks like he is watching a tennis match on TV. Then, quite quickly move your hand up just above your dog's head and then quickly down to the floor. If your dog loves the toy or treat you have, he may well jump into a 'down' position, at which point you can reward him with a "Good boy" and his treat. As before, you should reward for just trying, so if he only goes halfway down, give him a reward a few times, and then gradually wait a little longer until he goes further down before you reward him.

'Stand'

Teaching your puppy to stand might sound a bit pointless. Surely you only ever want your puppy to sit, right? Well, not so, mon ami.

You will need your puppy to 'stand', and you will be glad you taught him this trick when you take him for a check-up at the vet's, or if he's a dog that will need regular grooming.

Teaching your puppy to stand can be quite tricky, and it's even trickier if your dog doesn't do a reliable sit or a down yet, so make sure you teach *those* first.

One way to teach a puppy to stand is simply to 'lure' him into a standing position when he is sitting or lying down in front of you. I would experiment a little doing it from both a sitting *and* a lying-down position, and then go with the one your puppy more readily moves from.

If you can, start with your puppy sitting or lying across the front of you. So you should lure him into a sit or down so his nose is pointing in the direction your right (or left if you are doing it the other way) shoulder is facing. Then you take a treat and place it in front of his nose and then when he starts moving towards it to eat it, gradually move it away from him rising on the diagonal, so your puppy has to 'stand' up to get the treat.

You can reward him for just attempting to stand, so if he moves his body only slightly towards the treat, then tell him he is a 'good boy' and treat him. The next time you can wait until he moves his body slightly further into a stand position, then you gradually get him to stand and he enjoys the whole learning process.

Think back to when you were at school. You didn't just receive praise when you finished reading your first book. You were encouraged along the way. First you got a gold star for being able to read your ABCs. Then you started to put the letters together to spell words. C-A-T spells Cat (see how smart I am …). Then bigger words and sentences followed until finally you could read a short story.

Your dog is going through a similar process with everything he learns. So take your time, be lavish with praise, reward him for trying and enjoy the learning journey together.

'Touch'

One of the easiest ways to teach your puppy to stand is to teach him to hand touch. This means he 'touches' the palm of your hand with his nose. In fact, this particular trick can be used to teach your puppy all kinds of things from standing to heelwork. Let's do the hand touch basics and then show you how to teach your puppy to stand, using your hand as an example to get you started.

Teaching a 'hand touch' is also a good way to improve your timing when teaching tricks. Ideally you want to be verbally rewarding your dog with a 'good boy' as soon as he:

1. Plants his bum on the floor when doing a sit.
2. Places his chest on the floor when doing a down.
3. Or, in this case, as soon as his nose touches your hand.

The quicker you 'mark' the desired behaviour with some praise, the easier it will be for your dog to understand what you want him to do.

That's why this is such a good exercise to improve timing, because as soon as you feel his wet nose touch your hand you can say "Good boy".

Puppies are curious creatures, and yours probably won't need any encouragement to nose your hand when you present it to them, so let's try that first.

Start with your hands by your side or behind your back, and present one of your hands to your puppy holding it near his face.

He should move his head towards it and touch it with his nose. If he does then tell him he's a 'good boy' and give him a treat. If he doesn't then repeat five or six times and try moving your hand slightly closer to him.

If he still doesn't seem interested in touching you then try rubbing some kibble on your hands. Your puppy will usually smell the food and move towards it to investigate.

Then once he has got the idea, try doing it with the other hand. Then try presenting your hand ever so slightly further away from your puppy and he should reach towards it.

Once he is reliably touching both hands (which may take a day or two for him to master) then you can start adding the 'tell' or command, which in this case would be 'touch'.

Then you can start practising this all over the house, and outdoors in the garden too.

So hopefully you can see how you can use a touch to help you teach your dog to stand, but don't worry if you can't because I'm going to tell you anyway. Obviously you should ensure your dog is regularly touching your hand when you say "Touch" before you move onto this exercise.

So instead of luring your puppy into the standing position using a treat as we did in the last exercise, this time you would simply present your hand slightly above your puppy's head and wait for your puppy to move into a 'stand' position as he touches your hand.

Touch is also a great way to get your puppy used to the idea that human hands are friendly and nothing to fear, and it's also a great trick to help build your confidence if your puppy is a little shy.

'Spin'

I love 'spin', and I get my dogs to do it all the time when we are out and about. This trick looks great and dogs seem to love it too. Again think ASTR.

Attention – Show your dog the toy or treat. This trick is easier if your dog is standing up, and if he is a dog who likes to move away from you, then you should use a training lead to prevent him doing so.

Show – Show your dog what you want him to do. Hold the reward in front of his face. Imagine your dog is wearing a large top hat and slowly trace a circle around the outer brim of the hat. Your dog should follow your hand and circle round and return to something like the start position.

Tell – Say "Spin" once he has the idea, and you can lure him fully round quite easily.

Reward – This exercise usually takes a little while, and you should definitely be rewarding your dog for doing a quarter turn and then a half and eventually a full turn.

Take your time with this. A full 'spin' may take a few days or even a week to perfect, but there's no rush to get it done quickly. Once your dog is following the treat and spinning more easily, you should just use the hand movement to trace the circle, and then reward the dog afterwards. Then in time you can fade out the hand movement – you still say "Spin", but the hand movement is less defined. But this can take many weeks. Don't blame the dog if he doesn't do it straight away, and give him lots of praise when he starts to turn round. This will make him feel good.

Once you have locked down the 'spin', why not teach him a 'twist'? That's just spinning the opposite way round. So start the whole exercise again, and be prepared for it to take just as long as the 'spin' did.

Training tip:

It's much easier to teach a 'spin' from a standing position. However, if your dog keeps sitting down (which he might well do if that's what you have just taught him), move backwards slightly and tempt him towards you with the treat, then as he stands up and moves, you can start to trace the circle around his head. He will already be moving forward by then, and it's easier to get him to continue the movement but go around than it is to get him to start a 'spin' from a sitting position.

'Rollover'

Puppies are floppy little critters, and it's great fun seeing them do a rollover without even realising what just happened. It's also super easy to teach them to roll over, but you really do have to be patient and take your time when teaching your puppy a rollover, especially the first part of the exercise.

As you would imagine, you need to start this trick from a down position, and if you didn't imagine that then do so now, and make sure you wait until your puppy is reliably doing a down BEFORE you move onto a rollover.

So with your puppy lying in a down position in front of you, take a piece of kibble in your right hand, and hold it just in front of his nose so he stays in the down position.

I'm assuming now you are on your knees with your puppy lying down in front of you, facing you. You are going to use your right hand to get your puppy to roll over. Eventually, he is going to roll onto his right shoulder, and roll from right to left in front of you, as you are looking at him.

Start by slowly moving the treat from his nose down the side of his mouth and under his right ear. Your puppy should follow your hand and start turning his head as if he is looking behind his ear. Then slowly move your hand with the treat in behind your dog's ear and over the back/top of his head. You really do need to do this quite slowly. The idea is for your puppy to look behind as he follows the treat, and then as he follows the treat he flops over onto his side, and then he rolls over as he follows your hand as it moves over what would have been the back of his neck, but is now the front of his face, because he's rolled onto his back.

Some dogs get this trick straight away, but for others it can take a bit longer, so don't worry if he doesn't get it as quick as he did the others.

Troubleshooting trick tip

If you move your hand around the back of his head too quickly he will probably start turning his head to the left and following you, but then snap his head round the other way to grab the treat as it comes over his head.

It's a good idea to break this trick down into four sections.

Part one is to get your puppy to simply look left as your hand moves down the side of his face. Do 'just' this part five or six times rewarding with a tiny piece of kibble each time.

Then in **part two** you can start to reward your puppy with a "Good boy" as he flops onto his shoulder. Repeat this four or five times, then have a short break and tell your puppy how clever he is.

For **part three** you can offer the praise and reward as your puppy rolls full onto his back (with his paws in the air).

And finally, in **part four**, you can reward your puppy as he fully rolls over onto the other side. Drop the treat on the floor in front of him and give him a big old cuddle.

Then once your puppy is doing a full rollover, you can start to add the command 'over' as you lure him over.

That's a rollover done. Hurrah!

'Through the legs'

This is another really easy trick, and I like it because it is a fun way to encourage your puppy to come back to you.

You can use a toy or a treat, which you should first show your dog to get his attention. Then take a step back if you need to get your dog moving forwards and following the reward, and lure him towards you. Place your legs fairly wide apart but so you are comfortable, no full or half splits please … Then drop the toy or treat just between your legs and reward your dog with lots of praise when he picks it up. Repeat this a few times, gradually dropping the toy further behind your legs so your dog has to gradually move further underneath you to get it. Then when he is moving through, you can say "Under" or "In there" or whatever you want your TELL command to be.

Training tip:

Always put your hand straight between your legs as you drop the toy or food, and don't go around the side of your body and drop it behind, or your dog will just follow your hand around your body.

Also, don't throw the toy or treat too far between your legs and behind you either. Your dog will probably just run around you to get the toy.

After a few days' practising, you should be able to direct your dog between your legs using the command and the action of pretending you are throwing the toy between your legs. Then once your dog runs through, he will look for the toy on the floor, which you will then throw to him and give him lots of praise and affection.

So that's my super seven tricks to start you off. I have picked these because they are fairly easy to teach and I do them myself every day with my own and my clients' dogs.

All of the tricks require your dog to be fairly close to you, so when you practise them you are giving your dog a reason to be near you wherever you are.

We will go into your dog's nose a little later (not literally), but outside there is more air movement and, especially if you live in the UK, more moisture. Scent is essentially moisture, and your dog's nose is going to pick up many more scents than yours. These smells will be interesting to him, and he will want to explore them. This is why you need to spend a lot of time playing indoors and building up a drive that counteracts his desire to want to go and explore every smell that isn't you and your toy.

Tricks have real practical applications too. A great 'trick' you can use to help your puppy learn how to behave around new people is to get them to demonstrate a trick with your puppy. Sometimes family members and friends can be a real pain in the ass when they visit as they can 'undo' a lot of the good training you are putting in place. That is unless you put some rules in place …

A great thing to do is to make everyone pass a 'training test' before they can fuss and cuddle the puppy.

While your puppy is in the crate, let the visitor in and explain to them that the puppy gets a little excited when he meets new people so you need them to make him do a sit and a down before they can cuddle him.

Then give them a treat, let your puppy out of his crate and you show them how to do it first. Then it's their turn. Make sure they do a sit first and then a down; then they can pat the puppy on the head and tell him he's a 'good boy'.

This routine might sound a little draconian but it really works because it imposes a bit of structure at a time when your puppy is going to be mega excited to meet someone. It also teaches him to meet and greet people sitting or lying on the floor, and if he's sitting and lying on the floor then he isn't jumping up!

One of my clients did this when their extended family of eight people turned up. He had them stand in a circle, and one by one each made Charlie the giant schnauzer puppy do a sit and a down. He behaved perfectly afterwards.

This is a great self-esteem boost for the visitor too because they are helping with the training. If you still feel odd, just blame me and say this is what 'Dom the Dog Trainer' said you had to do, so you are doing it.

You will also be using these tricks to get your dog to focus on you while you are out socialising him, so let's move onto socialising and how to do it properly.

Summary

- Use ASTR to help you whenever you teach your puppy a trick or anything new. If he looks at you blankly, he is not being awkward; he either doesn't know what you want him to do, the reward you are using isn't rewarding enough or it's too complicated for him. Either way 'it's not the dog's fault', so take it back a few steps or break down the exercise and make it easier for him.

- Don't make the mistake of thinking tricks are just something dog trainers do. These tricks will give your puppy something to focus on when you are socialising him. Teaching him some tricks will make it easier for you to distract him from the thing you don't want him to do. Tricks are great fun, and you will surprise yourself by how clever you and your dog really are once you start practising them.

BONUS – To help you master these tricks I've included my Clicker-Free Trick Training Course in the resources. This is a short course that will teach you five of the tricks taught in this chapter. To get full and immediate access to this FREE course go to:

www.mydogssuperhero.com/perfectpuppyproject

Chapter 8

How to Socialise Your Puppy

"I remember you being a lot bigger." Peter Pan

"To a ten-year-old I'm huge …" Captain Hook

The foggy screen clears and the picture focuses in on a newborn baby being held by her proud parents. Then a cartoon girl with blue hair wearing a simple green dress walks view. She is also watching the baby on a big television screen. We watch as the mother names the baby Riley, and the father proudly calls her his 'little bundle of joy'.

The father's words create the feel-good moment which triggers the first memory to be produced in Riley's brain, and the girl with blue hair, who we now learn is Joy, stores the memory safely away in Riley's memory bank.

That's the opening scene from the Disney Pixar movie *Inside Out*. The film follows five personified emotions, Joy, Sadness, Fear, Disgust and Anger, who influence Riley's actions via a control console in her brain.

The premise of the film is not too dissimilar to an old cartoon I used to read in *The Beano*, called The Numskulls, which is maybe why I enjoyed it so much.

As Riley grows up all of her experiences become memories, stored in coloured orbs which are sent into her long-term memory bank each night. Her five most important core memories (which are all happy ones) are housed in a hub, and each core memory powers an aspect of her personality.

Now, obviously, neither we nor our dogs have little men and women running around in our brains controlling our every move, but this idea of 'core memories' is a relevant one.

I can vaguely remember stupidly running in front of a car when I was five years old and I broke my leg. I can only replay brief snapshots of the immediate aftermath, but the 4-inch scar running across my ankle is a permanent reminder of the incident.

I can more clearly remember getting into a fight on my first day of school with a boy called Philip, who would later become my best friend. We were both a little eager to put the chairs away after storytime and ended up fighting over the last chair, and we were sent to see the headmaster for our troubles.

You will have a bunch of these core memories too. Some of them may be painful to think about, but hopefully most of them are pleasant. These memories and experiences, both good *and* bad, make us who we are.

And although *Inside Out* is just a movie, it has its roots based in truth. The director, Pete Docter, first began developing the film in 2010, after noticing changes in his daughter's personality as she grew older. The film's producers consulted numerous psychologists including Dacher Keltner from the University of California, Berkeley, who helped revise the story by emphasising the neuropsychological findings that **human emotions affect interpersonal relationships** and can be significantly moderated by them.

Author C J Heck put it more simply when she said *"We are all products of our environment; every person we meet, every new experience or adventure, every book we read, touches and changes us, making us the unique being we are."*

And so it is with our dogs.

The dog you own in six months' time is very much a product of all the experiences he goes through now as a puppy.

This is why ensuring your dog is properly and adequately socialised, within the recommended time frame, is crucial if you want him to develop into a well-adjusted and easy-to-look-after dog.

I've presented to you what I think is the easiest way to get your dog into an easy-to-manage routine at home, with the **Play, Eat, Sleep, Repeat** routine, and you also have a play and training routine to enable you to bond and build a great connection with your dog.

Now, it's time for us to talk about one of the most misunderstood aspects of puppy training, socialisation.

What it *is*, what it *isn't* and *why* it's so important.

How to screw up your puppy

Socialisation is probably the main area mistakes are made due to bad advice given to inexperienced puppy owners, who usually end up going down two ill-advised routes.

The first bit of bad advice usually comes from your puppy's vet.

Socialisation myth number one

'You should keep your puppy indoors until he has finished his injections.'

Now, I love vets dearly; they do an unbelievable job in incredibly difficult circumstances and are always dealing with time pressures. This maybe explains why some vets are rushed into giving blanket recommendations about socialisation and tell owners not to take their puppies for walks until after the puppy's second injection date. This leads to most puppy owners not taking their puppy outside at all until the puppy is 13 weeks old, sometimes later.

This is a huge mistake that *will* stunt your puppy's social development and can often lead to nervous puppies developing into fearful dogs.

Personally, I allow my puppy onto the ground outdoors in areas where I know it's clean. It's fine for you not to do that, but you can and should be carrying your puppy outside and showing him the big, wide world, even if he is a large breed and even if it's raining, snowing or blowing a gale.

Socialisation myth number two

'Socialisation is about teaching your puppy to play with other dogs.'

This second BIG socialisation myth comes from well-meaning but clueless dog owners, *and* some dog trainers, who insist socialisation is all about your puppy meeting and playing with lots of other dogs and puppies. And socialisation isn't and shouldn't be about that, at all.

If you teach your puppy other dogs are the most interesting thing in the world, and encourage him to play with them at every opportunity, then he will seek them out whenever you step outside your front door. This usually leads to pulling, whining, lunging and barking behaviours *on* lead, and a total lack of control over your puppy *off* lead, because he's obsessed with running off to find other dogs to play with.

Remember, dogs learn by doing and they will seek out activities that they enjoy.

Put them together, and these two socialisation fuck-ups, I mean … erm, myths, contribute massively to the number of out-of-control dogs we see today, many of whom end up in rescue centres.

The socialisation disaster recipe

So the vet recommends your puppy stays at home for three weeks, which stops him from experiencing and getting used to the neighbourhood he lives in. Then the first proactive thing the owner does is take the puppy to the park (or a puppy party) where the puppy learns to be a bully to, or be bullied by, other dogs.

Not ideal, I'm sure you will agree.

So, what should you do instead?

Follow my foolproof socialisation programme, of course!

So let's begin.

When to start socialising your puppy

You should make a start on your puppy's socialisation as soon as you bring him home. Don't think it's OK to wait until he is a bit bigger and more confident; it isn't.

Seriously, this *can't* wait. Some dogs never get over the fearfulness which could have been avoided with proper socialisation.

The socialisation schedule

You can split the socialisation schedule into two periods. The first is when your puppy has just arrived at his new home but he's unable to go for 'normal walks' because of his puppy injections. The second is when he is able to walk on the lead alongside you, which will happen after he's finished his injections in three or four weeks' time.

These injections are important as they will help to ensure your puppy doesn't catch any nasty potentially fatal diseases.

But just as important is inoculating your puppy from becoming a fearful dog, which you do by gradually exposing him to many different experiences.

Let's take a look at how you can begin safely socialising your puppy instead of placing him under a 'no walks' house arrest.

And it's actually a good thing your puppy can't be walked just yet because it means he can experience his first taste of the outside world from safely inside your coat. Yes, for the first couple of weeks, you get to carry your puppy everywhere you go, and carrying means cuddling. Yay!

Observational socialisation

This is where I would start when socialising your puppy. For the first few days, and maybe the first week depending on how confident your puppy is, I would make 'observing' the main aim of all your interactions. So you can progress from taking your puppy from your front street to the park, beach, woods, supermarket and school gates to pick your kids up, and the main aim is to make sure your puppy is happy observing and is comfortable with everything he sees.

Some mild stress is fine, but it's easy to miss the vital signs your puppy is stressed out, especially when you are a new owner. Don't try to force your puppy to do anything at this early stage. You are all your puppy has to protect him from the big bad world, so be a responsible, watchful and careful owner.

As the first week progresses you will see your puppy grow in confidence and become less bothered by all the new and different sights, smells and sounds.

Here's a socialisation diary to help you through the first few days.

Socialisation example: day one

The first day you bring your puppy home from the breeder is going to be pretty overwhelming for him anyway, so it's totally fine to just spend three or four 10-minute sessions with him in your front garden, watching the world go by. In fact, you'll be spending a lot of time outside with him doing toilet breaks, so you can combine a toilet trip with a 'neighbourhood watch' session.

Socialisation example: day two

On day two take your puppy for a short carry (not a walk) around your immediate neighbourhood.

This can be as simple as a slow 10-minute jaunt around the block.

This might not seem like a lot of time, but apart from when you brought him home, this is maybe the first time your puppy has spent any extended period of time outdoors.

And this is a huge deal for your puppy, who smells and hears a lot more than he sees. Your puppy will not only be looking at trees you walk past, but he will also be smelling the individual scent from the leaves, bark and any animals living in (or who have walked past and peed on) the tree.

I imagine for our puppies going outdoors for the first time it is like the scene from *The Wizard of Oz*, when Dorothy's house crash-lands on the wicked witch, and she emerges from a black-and-white existence into glorious technicolour.

Your puppy goes from only smelling the safe, dry (and boring) smells inside your house to the exciting, vibrant variety of ever-changing smells in the outdoors.

Let him soak it all up, and if you meet anyone who wants to say hello to your puppy, ask them to hold their hand out so he can smell it first. If he moves towards them and is curious then tell them they can stroke his chest and chin with the back of their hand, but don't allow people to overwhelm your puppy.

Socialisation example: day three

Today you can head out a little further, or a better idea might be to take him a short distance in your car. Take him somewhere different (even slightly different is good), and again carry him around and let him watch the world go by.

Getting your puppy used to travelling

I highly recommend you get your puppy used to being in the car from day one (or day two). Many puppies end up afraid of travelling, or suffering from travel sickness, because their only two early experiences of travel were when they were plucked from their canine families and taken to a new home, and then a day later taken to the vet's to be roughly handled and jabbed.

Make an effort to ensure your puppy travels in the car regularly, and that it's enjoyable for him. It's totally fine to carry him for the first few sessions in the car and then progress to a travel harness or crate.

Socialisation example: day four

On your fourth socialisation saunter you can carry your puppy a little further than yesterday if you wish; the main thing is he sees lots of things on the walk. So walk past lots of buses, lorries, people, lollipop ladies and even other animals.

The main thing to remember is all of these interactions must go at the puppy's own pace. We want your puppy to have lots of experiences, but we also want those experiences to be (for the most part) positive ones.

You are the one who controls, or who *should* control, the dynamic of the interactions he makes, which will ultimately determine how well socialised he is.

This means you need to be a selfish owner and put the needs of your puppy **before** the wants and wishes of random people you meet. They may want to cuddle, stroke or introduce their dog to your puppy, and if you let them then some of those people will think it's OK to pounce on your puppy without permission, so don't allow this to happen.

Your aim is to make your puppy feel safe at all times. If he feels safe then his tiny brain will be in the perfect state to more easily absorb all the new experiences you are exposing him to.

You will likely be carrying your puppy for the first couple of weeks anyway, and holding the puppy means you can much more easily control where he goes. But you also need to control what comes into the puppy's space, so use this script to help you handle interactions with overbearing, pushy puppy lovers. It goes like this:

"Hey there, I'm socialising my puppy and I wonder if you can help me. I want him to meet people, but not to be too overwhelmed, so if you would like to say hello, then I need you to hold out your hand towards him and wait until he sniffs it, then if he is happy you can stroke his chest and chin."

Simples.

This is a great exercise to do because it gives the other person clear instructions how they should approach your puppy, and you can correct them if they go 'off-script' and try cuddling, sniffing and crowding him.

It also gets you used to the idea that you are in charge of your puppy. A lot of the training I've taught you so far actually goes against what most puppy owners will be doing with *their* dogs. To keep your puppy safe requires you to be a selfish owner, and this means you are going to have to grow some balls (or ladyballs) if you are going to do right by your puppy. There's no better time to start this process than the first couple of times you take him out.

Continue this steady observational routine for the next 10 days, and as your puppy gets more confident you can allow him to get closer to all the things, people and animals he meets.

But what exactly should your puppy be seeing on your socialisation walks? Ah, for that we need a list …

The Socialisation Checklist

My wife, Beth, loves lists. She lives by lists she writes for work and for personal stuff. In fact, I'm sure she has a list about her lists.

I myself work better when I have a list too. When I'm going to the gym I have a list of exercises I'm doing that particular day, and without a shopping list to follow I would just end up buying chocolate, magazines and cookies. Even today I have three things on my 'to-do' list.

1. Write socialisation chapter.
2. Sketch out Worry Free Walks seminar.
3. Meet a client.

Why you need a list

Lists make it easy to remember the tasks we need to complete. And lists can be very useful when we are talking about socialisation.

The idea of having a list of sights and experiences you and your dog 'tick off' together has fallen out of fashion with many dog trainers, but personally I think this is a mistake.

I totally agree the *quality* of the socialisation is more important than the *quantity* of things your puppy is exposed to, but I don't see why dispensing with a list helps anyone, least of all the first-time puppy owner this book has been written for.

Not everything on the list is a 'must-see' experience, and if you live in Australia then you might want your dog to see more kangaroos than horses, but the basic premise is the same no matter where in the world you live.

And to continue the shopping list analogy, it isn't the end of the world if you forget an item, or miss something out of your socialisation schedule. Use this checklist simply as a guide.

Think of the Socialisation Checklist like a game of Pokémon GO, only instead of seeking out Charmander and Squirtle you are on the trail with Socialasaur (your dog), and your mission is to tick off the list all the things you want your puppy to be OK with when he grows up.

Puppy owners often get overwhelmed with the amount of experiences a puppy need to 'cross off the list', but it needn't be so stressful.

Structuring the socialisation

Here's a simple list of experiences you should give your puppy in the first few weeks:

Carry your puppy down your street (do this daily) – This will expose your puppy to cars, people, dogs, birds and hopefully noisy buses and lorries too. If you live somewhere more secluded then you need to get off your arse and travel to where there are noisy buses and lorries.

Visit a friend's house – Spending the afternoon at a friend's house is a great way to build your puppy's confidence. Pick a sensible friend who isn't going to shriek and wail like a teenager at a Justin Bieber concert when they see your puppy. Take the crate along with you and allow your puppy to spend some time in and out of the crate, and in your friend's garden. You can keep control using the house lead you've been using in your own house. Also, try to seek out someone who has an older, calmer dog that your puppy can learn to be around, but not play with; again keeping your puppy on a house lead will give you more control and not allow him to annoy the other dog.

A trip to town – Even a short trip to your local town, village or city centre will provide lots of opportunities for your puppy to see all kinds of things. Think about it; on one trip your puppy will likely see dozens of cars, people, birds, other dogs and, crucially, he will get to experience the general hustle and bustle of a busy town centre. It's totally cool to take a little break and sit on a bench to allow your puppy to process what he's seen, or better yet, enjoy …

A trip to a pub or café – These are my favourite trips, especially if there's a hot chocolate or, even better, a pint of Black Sheep for me to enjoy. When he is small and easier to control it's the ideal time to get your puppy used to doing things you want him to do well when he is an older dog, and the more places you are able to take your well-behaved dog the more time you can spend with him.

A trip to the groomer's – You may not have a dog who needs to be groomed regularly, but there's no harm in taking him to the groomer s anyway just to meet the groomer (who will usually be a more sensible human stooge than a regular dog lover). There will be different smells and sounds in the salon for him to enjoy and get used too. If your puppy is a breed of dog that needs regular grooming when he is older, then I would recommend popping in your local groomer's at least weekly to get him used to being there. Some of these visits can be very brief pop-ins, and you can take a couple of treats along with you which the groomer can feed him, which will help them bond more quickly.

A trip to the vet's – Even if your dog doesn't need grooming, you **will** need to get him used to going to the vet's. Hopefully you have been handling your puppy at home regularly and teaching him to 'stand', which will help the vet more easily examine him, but you still should be popping in your vet's every other week just to get him used to the clinical environment. At the very least you should pop into the vet's a couple of days after the initial visit when your puppy got checked over and given his jabs. This second visit should be low-stress, and just involve some treats given to him by the vet's receptionist.

And that's a simple socialisation plan anyone can do no matter where you live, or what kind of breed of dog you've acquired.

This chapter covers observational socialisation, but what happens when you start walking your puppy on lead? Well, the truth is this is where the socialisation plan can go pear shaped (or tits-up, depending on your choice of words).

So, in the next chapter we are going to look at how you should handle off-lead and on-lead interactions with your puppy so you can enjoy stress-free trips to the park.

Summary

- Puppy socialisation is simple to understand but easy to get wrong. You will stay on track by always putting the needs of your puppy before anyone else's needs, even your own. Your puppy needs to experience lots of new sights, smells and sounds before he is 14 weeks old, but this doesn't mean he needs to have them forced upon him all at once. It does mean, however, you need to head outdoors with your puppy daily even if you are carrying him everywhere for a few weeks.

- You are your puppy's protector and guardian, so for dog's sake, act like it. Don't allow overzealous strangers to crowd your puppy and shatter his fragile confidence. Give them rules and if they can't follow them, then put the needs of your puppy first; hold your hand up to them and say no, and then walk away. Follow this plan and your puppy's confidence will grow massively within the first few days.

- A dog training friend of mine has three words written on the puppy packs she gives away in her training classes. They are, Out, Out, Out. You simply have to get your puppy outside experiencing the world straight away. Do not make the mistake of thinking just because your puppy can't go for 'walks' until he has finished his inoculations, he can't go outside at all. He can go out, he should go out and he needs to go out. Your puppy needs you to literally carry him through this early socialisation period, and help him grow into a confident dog.

BONUS – To help guide you through this tricky socialisation period I've got a downloadable Socialisation Checklist and Safe Socialisation Training Video which show you how to gradually expose your puppy to the new experiences he needs to see, without overwhelming him and making him fearful. To get access to these bonuses go to:

www.mydogssuperhero.com/perfectpuppyproject

Chapter 9

How to Be the 'Park Leader' Your Puppy Wants to Follow

"Dogs are blameless, devoid of calculation, neither blessed, nor cursed with human motives. They can't really be held responsible for what they do. But we can."

Jon Katz

One of the most satisfying parts of my job is demonstrating with my cocker spaniel, Sidney, at the dog training seminars I deliver all over the UK. Attendees often comment on how he wags his tail the whole time we are working and never takes his eyes off me.

Sid hardly ever wanders away from me, even when people are calling for him (or eating biscuits he might like). We have lots of tricks we perform, but it's his focus on me that impresses the audience the most.

This makes me proud because that's exactly what I wanted him to be like when I got him. See, at the time we got Sid we had an older dog, Barry, and a dog walking and boarding business, but I didn't want Sid to get too attached to other dogs. I didn't want him to be frightened of them, but neither did I want him to be overly interested in them.

I had a goal to have a dog who thinks the sun shines out of my arse, and my purposeful actions have led me there.

This purposeful action never stops either. At a seminar I did just last week, someone helping out with the organising seemed concerned that Sid was in his cage a lot and suggested I let him out to wander around the hall and stretch his legs. I politely declined of course.

If I allow him to wander the hall on his own, do you think that will make him easier or more difficult to control when we do our demonstration. I think we both know the answer …

And when you are socialising your puppy, you should always be asking yourself *"Is what I am doing now going to help or hinder me in my quest to develop this puppy into a great dog?"* And if it isn't going to help, then don't do it!

We have come to the time in your puppy's life when he is able to go for proper walks outside. How exciting!

Proper puppy walks

Proper walks for your puppy means all four paws are on the floor, which also means his nose and mouth are a lot closer to anything and everything that he finds interesting. And because of their superior sniffing powers, dogs and puppies can get easily intrigued by the most mundane things.

Lamp posts and bushes top the list, but there is a plethora of pavement perfumes your puppy will find very alluring on his walks.

And that's just stationary obstacles and things lying around on the ground. Your puppy will be even more fascinated by living, breathing and moving creatures like cats, dogs, kids and birds, who are lying in wait and ready to distract him at every turn …

Preparing for a puppy walk

To help you stay in control it's a good idea to take with you on your walks a small bag of your dog's kibble, with a few treats mixed in (or small pieces of cheese or hot dogs). This will make the regular kibble more tempting.

I would also advise you to take one of your puppy's favourite toys with you whenever you take him out. He may not be hungry but he can almost always be tempted to play, especially if you have been practising games with him at home.

Arming yourself with your puppy's favourite toys and treats means you will be more easily able to get him to focus and look at you when there are other distractions around, and there WILL be lots of distractions outside.

The Perfect Puppy Project

Short walks for little legs

Your puppy needs short walks for a reason. Depending on the breed, your puppy's body and his bones are still developing until he's around two years old. Growth plates sitting at the end of his bones don't close until around 18 months, and until then they are soft and vulnerable to injury. One of the most common causes of these injuries is repetitive exercise with a young puppy. So, until he's around 18 months old, long on-lead walks and hikes are out of the question and should be replaced with short mooching, sniffing and playing sessions on walks with you. Hurrah!

The really good news is all the playing and training you've been doing indoors, and the socialising you've been doing outdoors, mean your puppy will confidently handle the distractions he encounters on the walk and be perfectly primed to play with you when you entice him with his toys and treats.

The socialisation exploration

In the last chapter we concentrated on observational socialisation, which involved your puppy mainly watching everything from the comfort and safety of your arms. He was taking in the world around him and getting used to being comfortable with all the different noises, scents and movements present in your local town.

These form the 'core memories' now locked away in your puppy's brain, and these core memories provide a reference point for the explorational experiences he is going to have from now on.

Now, we move onto more of an exploration and interaction phase, which brings new challenges …

For example, because he is walking on the ground, your puppy is closer to the action, which may mean he sometimes reacts differently to how he did when you were carrying him.

That's fine and to be expected. What you shouldn't start doing now is forcing your puppy to interact with anything he is uncomfortable with.

I sometimes see new puppy owners dragging their puppy out from under a park bench to meet a dog or person because they feel the puppy 'has to get used to people and dogs'. He does, of course, but *not* like that. This kind of experience can severely knock your puppy's confidence. You've essentially gone from being your puppy's protector to the pushy mother (or father) who chucks their kid in at the deep end.

Allow your puppy to move forward, explore and meet people at his own pace.

However, sometimes problems can occur at the other end of the scale, when your puppy is too excitable, desperate to meet and even chase or jump up at everyone he encounters on a walk.

In this instance, it's just as important you keep good control of your puppy and don't allow him to learn bad behaviours you'll find difficult to fix later.

Protecting your puppy

Just because your puppy is now on the ground doesn't mean to say you stop looking out for him, and you especially need to take care when pain-in-the-arse dog owners turn up with their out-of-control dogs.

I'm not a fan of owners who permanently pick up their puppies whenever they show the slightest sign of unease, but you should take all necessary steps to prevent a crazy dog from barging into your small puppy. Stand in the way, or by all means pick up your puppy if that happens, and walk away. It's probably not even worth saying anything to the stupid owner, although I must admit, I have been known to utter a few choice words rhyming with cupid stunt.

It's much easier to stop your puppy from wandering off, jumping up at people or pulling to get away from you by simply teaching him something else to do instead. And the good news is you've already taught your puppy a bunch of tricks which you can now practise outdoors.

Getting your puppy's attention outdoors

A lot of what you do with your puppy at the park, beach and woods is actually the same as what you taught him at home.

You simply teach your puppy to sit, lie down and play games, which will keep his focus firmly on you, and off the dogs, rabbits, squirrels and pigeons that would otherwise tempt him away from you.

Don't just assume, though, that because your puppy sits, spins and rolls over at home that he will do the same thing at the park. You almost always have to reteach your puppy to listen, play and interact with you in each new location you take him. After a few repetitions he will remember that the park is the place he does fun things with you, but you'll have to up your energy levels to convince him initially.

The stop-and-sniff saunter

A regular short 'walk' for your young puppy should consist of some walking, training, sniffing and playing.

Let's break those down.

Start your walk by showing your puppy some of the toys and treats you have. You can play a little game and practise a few tricks before you even leave the house. I call this pre-exhausting the puppy.

Practice makes perfect so remember to practise lots of sits and downs with your puppy on your walk. It's sensible to teach your puppy to do a sit every time you go to cross the road, but you can also ask him to do a sit, a down or a stand at every lamppost you pass. Regularly interacting with your puppy like this reminds him you are still there, and you have things he likes.

You can teach your puppy to walk alongside you by using kibble (or treats) to keep him focused on you while you are walking. If he wanders too far ahead simply stop walking, call his name and lure him back alongside you, all the while talking to him, and praising him when he walks beside you.

Remember to allow your puppy some time to sniff and explore his surroundings. You have magazines, Facebook and Netflix to entertain you; well, your puppy needs to check his 'pee-mail' to find out what's going on in the neighbourhood.

When it comes to passing by people and other dogs I would recommend you teach your puppy to look at you and sit whenever another dog approaches; again use the toys and treats you are carrying. You can also teach your puppy to look at the treats you are carrying as you pass by the other dog owner.

Your puppy is always learning, and you are teaching him. This is what we do when we see other dogs and people; we simply carry on as normal.

Controlling your puppy in the park

I like to teach my puppy I am the most interesting thing at the park, and I do this by playing games with him. First find a quiet area of the park away from kids, dogs and any other distractions.

I recommend you attach a 2-metre soft lead to your puppy's collar. This 'safety net' will help you:

a.   Prevent your puppy from becoming distracted and wandering off.
b.   Keep him near you while you teach him to play re-trieve, tuggy and find-it games, outdoors.

Then start playing with your dog using the toys and treats to get his attention and focus on you.

You will probably need to up your energy levels to get your puppy looking at you. Even if there are no dogs, birds or kids around there is still a multitude of smells and sounds that your puppy will find distracting. This is where a squeaky toy, or some small pieces of chopped-up cheese or hot dogs, come in very handy.

Remember, the more distracting the environment, the higher value the treats need to be, and the more effort and energy you need to put into the game you are playing to get your dog's attention.

Once your puppy is looking at you, you can play the same food and toy games from chapters 5 and 6, and then when he is warmed up try practising the tricks from chapter 7.

I do have one new game for you to play in the park and it's guaranteed to get your distracted puppy laser-focused on you.

The catch-up game

This game can be played with food or toys as well as affection, and it encourages your puppy to run towards you, which I'm sure you'll agree is a very desirable and useful behaviour.

Take a small handful of treats and show your puppy one of the pieces, then throw the treat a metre or two away, making sure your puppy sees it being thrown.

Your puppy should go and retrieve the treat from the ground. Then just as he eats it, you call his name in your happy dog voice, and as he comes towards you, wave another treat at him.

As he gets near to you, throw that treat to the side of you furthest away from the direction he is coming from. Again, not too far away, you want him to get the reward. As soon as he collects the treat or toy, call his name again.

As he gets quicker, you can increase the distance you throw the treat. Also, as he is retrieving the treat, you can walk in the opposite direction, so he has a bit further to come to you.

When your puppy has the idea, you can start mixing it up a bit. Every third or fourth go, don't throw a treat, and instead, when he gets to you praise him, stroke his ears and tell him what a brilliant dog he is.

Then start the game again, and this time on the third go, when he is retrieving the thrown treat, say his name, and when he comes towards you, have three treats ready in your hand to reward him with.

Dogs are eternal chancers, and mixing up the rewards like this will keep him guessing as to what he is going to get next.

Bingo! You now have a puppy you can't get rid of who follows you around the park like you're the Pied Piper!

For a more comprehensive puppy play-park routine, I would recommend you grab a copy of *Worry Free Walks*, the first book in the Street-Smart Dog Training series, which you can get from Amazon, Audible or direct from me at:

www.mydogssuperhero.com/worryfreewalks

Summary

- Walks with your young puppy aren't about long, boring on-lead army-style marches. In fact, long walks are bad for your puppy's delicate bones and should be avoided. Instead, you are going to teach your puppy to walk nicely by your side, as you explore the world together. Give him time to explore, absorb and process the world he lives in, and continue to build on the excellent observational socialisation you did in the previous chapter.

- Be prepared when you head out for a walk with your puppy. Take some kibble and treats, and always take a toy with you as well. Every time you come to a patch of grass or paved area, get your toy out and show it to your puppy. Get him excited, and when he's looking at you, ask him to do a sit or a down, and then reward him with the toy. These mini 'play-dates' will be what your puppy remembers from the walks, and he will look forward to playing them again next time you take him out.

- Socialising your puppy at the park, beach and woods is about teaching him 'This is what we do here'. This means you have to do stuff with him. Passive owners have poorly behaved puppies, and active owners have happy attentive puppies. The long lead you are using stops your puppy from getting distracted and running away from you, and the toys, treats and games you play will help keep him glued to your side.

Chapter 10

Your Next 90-Day Puppy Plan

"I call it the art of fighting, without fighting".

Bruce Lee

On the first page of her seminal dog training book *Don't Shoot the Dog!*, author Karen Pryor says:

"Behaviour that is already occurring, no matter how sporadically, can always be intensified with positive reinforcement. If you call a puppy, and it comes, and you pet it, the pup's coming when called will be more reliable even without any other training."

That nicely and neatly sums up how I think you should approach all the interactions you have with and all the experiences you give your new puppy.

By playing with your puppy often and everywhere, you will teach him, through positive reinforcement, **you** are a cool cat who is worth hanging around with. This means you will end up with a dog who prefers being with you over anything else he encounters.

This means you need to treat every trip to the park as an opportunity to prove to your puppy you are the most fun person in the world. Or, as I like to call it, BMFI.

How to BMFI

You can Be More Fucking Interesting by playing and interacting with your puppy, using the simple games, tricks and exercises I've laid out in this book.

Some fluffy-bunny dog trainers have a huge stick up their arse when they hear me say 'Be more interesting'.

They scrunch up their confused little faces and say something like "That's not very good advice. What does *be more interesting* even mean?"

Well, it's about providing entertainment, play and fun for your dog, so he sees you as a fun guy (or gal) to be with. Do this often enough and he will look to you for guidance and entertainment, which means he enjoys and wants to spend time with you.

The fluffy bunnies can't get their head round that, because they don't look at dog ownership the way I do. They think a dog should have other doggy friends he plays and socialises with.

But as we've seen, this puts unrealistic expectations on the dog and makes way him harder to control.

By closely following the plan you are holding in your hands, by being a responsible owner and *not* allowing your dog to learn that other things are more interesting than you in the park, you will achieve the utopia for all dog owners, which is … a dog who is easy to look after.

Dog training without dog training

Is it really possible for you to train your puppy to love AND want to be with you by just playing and interacting with him?

Ya darn tootin' it is!

See, if your dog never learns that playing with other dogs is fun because he is too busy enjoying himself with you, then you will never have a recall problem, because he will always *want* to be with you.

If your dog never learns that chewing shoes and television controls is enjoyable because you either keep him in a crate when you are busy, or you have lots of tasty chew toys on hand to distract him with, then you will never have a destructive dog who damages your property.

If from a young age you correctly teach your dog that his crate is a safe space where good things happen, then he will never develop separation anxiety.

That's dog training *without* dog training.

I'm aware I'm painting quite an idealistic picture here and not everything you do with your puppy will go 100% to plan all the time, but you will be pleasantly surprised how well behaved your future dog is because of the decisions you made and actions you take with your puppy now, based on the teachings in this book.

Be disciplined

I don't mean be disciplined with your puppy; I mean be disciplined with yourself, and what you allow your puppy to enjoy.

Be disciplined when you first bring him home, and make sure he spends some time in his crate, and not every second cuddling on your lap.

Be disciplined with your housetraining and keep taking your puppy outside for a toilet break after every meal, drink and play session.

Be disciplined when you are socialising him, and don't allow clueless passers-by to ruin your puppy with their thoughtless handling.

Be disciplined when you are exercising and training your puppy at the park. It's tempting to see other dogs playing nicely and worry that your dog is somehow missing out by not joining in, but don't worry; he *isn't* missing out. You can provide everything your puppy needs.

Raising a puppy can be really hard work, and there will be times in the next few weeks and months when your puppy will severely test your patience and make you wonder if this is all too much for you.

When that happens just stick to the plan, and know the worst will be over in a couple of months' time. Of course, if you are really struggling then invest in a reputable dog trainer to come and help you get back on track.

And if you feel like you need it, then by all means do some formal training classes with your puppy. In fact, I would highly recommend you find a good training class where you can learn to do tricks, walk to heel, come back when called, etc. But, most of all, these classes should be teaching you how to bond with your puppy.

If the lesson you are attending becomes a free-for-all puppy play session where dogs are jumping all over each other, then pick your dog up and walk away.

Make life easy for yourself and stick as closely to the plan as you can, and remember, the strong bond you have with your puppy is the foundation stone on which your relationship is built.

To help you more easily implement the lessons in this book, I have included some cool video and audio bonuses which you can get access to in the following chapter.

Future training

When he's older, more mature and physically capable, there's a huge range of canine activities out there for your puppy to try, from scentwork, heelwork, agility, treibball, flyball and everything else in between. All of those activities will be a lot easier to teach if you can quickly get your puppy's attention because you have a great bond with him, and keeping your puppy safely beside you in a busy park is also a LOT easier when you are the object of his affections.

Allowing your puppy to regularly enjoy chasing birds, rabbits, dogs or people is one way to virtually guarantee he will grow up to be a dog who is easily distracted, and a pain in the arse to exercise off lead.

If you are unable to control your dog off lead, then you are going to have to exercise him on a long lead, or not allow him any off-leash exercise. This means you will struggle to get rid of your dog's energy on your daily walks, which makes destructive behaviours at home more likely.

Like most things in life, with dog training, prevention is better than cure, and you have a unique opportunity with your puppy to 'prevent' lots of the easy-to-make but potentially damaging training mistakes which often bring about heartache and stress for inexperienced puppy owners, and sadly lead to many dogs being given up by their exasperated guardians.

A lot of what I teach is about setting you up for success by creating a rock-solid relationship between you and your dog, and by minimising the chances of things going wrong.

Stay true to the path you've started on, and your puppy will grow up to be a loving and much-loved member of your family, and an awesome ambassador for pet dogs all over the world.

Have fun!

Thanks for reading, now turn the page for your free gift …

Your Special Free Gift

I hope this book was enjoyable to read, but most of all I hope it inspires you to do more with your puppy.

I appreciate there's only so much practical demonstration you can get from a book, so to help you move forward faster with your training, I am giving you access to **'The Perfect Puppy Project'** resources.

This series of free dog training masterclasses will add lots of meat to the bones of this book. You will see me demonstrate with my own and my clients' dogs the simple training techniques I have described here.

Inside the free resources you will get:

Bonus One , 'The Perfect Puppy Shopping List' – I can almost guarantee you'll end up getting too many soft toys that are more suitable for human babies, and not enough practical treat-dispensing toys that will entertain your puppy and give him an outlet for his chewing habits.

Bonus Two , 'The Puppy Primer Audio Training' – To help make the first few days with your puppy as easy and stress free as possible I've put together a Puppy Primer Audio Training, which you can listen to at home or on the go, from your phone, computer or tablet. In this two-hour bonus training I pick out the key points from the book and give case study examples that show you how to quickly settle your new puppy into a stress-free routine.

Bonus Three, 'Puppy Food Games Masterclass ' – To help you further master 'using the food' I've put together a Puppy Food Games Masterclass which will more clearly demonstrate a lot of the food games I talked about in chapter 5.

Bonus Four, 'Clicker-Free Trick Training Course ' – To help you master the tricks in chapter 7, I've include full access to my Clicker-Free Trick Training Course. This is a short course that will show you how to quickly teach your puppy five cool tricks.

Bonus Five, 'Safe Socialisation Checklist and Videos' – To help guide you through the tricky socialisation period, I've got a downloadable Socialisation Checklist and a Safe Socialisation Training Video which show you how to gradually expose your puppy to the new experiences he needs to see, without overwhelming him and making him fearful.

To get FREE, full and immediate access to this 'must-see' puppy training masterclass go to:

www.mydogssuperhero.com/perfectpuppyproject

Discussion guide for dog trainers and puppy owners

My wish is *The Perfect Puppy Project* helps first-time dog owners build an amazing relationship with their puppies, so fewer out-of-control dogs end up in rescue centres all over the world.

We need to become a more responsible dog owning community putting the needs of our dogs above and beyond any selfish needs we may have.

I firmly believe if you raise your puppy the way I have described in this book, then you will more likely end up with a dog who looks to you, the owner, for fun, enjoyment and pleasure, and not birds, squirrels, rabbits and other dogs, all things which, when desired by the dog, take him *away* from the owner.

So, I encourage puppy owners and dog trainers to discuss the methods taught in this book, to ensure that the needs of pet dog owners are met by the dog training taught in church halls and community centres all over the world.

I'll help kick off the debate with the series of questions below. The first three are general, and the second three are more pertinent to the content in this book.

1. What was the purpose of this book? (e.g. to teach, to entertain)
2. If this book was intended to teach the reader something, did it succeed? Was something learned from

reading this book? If so, what? If not, why did the book fail as a teaching tool?

3. Was there a specific passage that had left an impression, good or bad? Share the passage and its effect.

4. What does socialisation mean to the first-time puppy owner, the dog trainer, your puppy?

5. Is it more important to train your puppy with food or toys?

6. What does it mean to the new puppy owner to have an 'easy-to-look-after dog' and what are the biggest challenges a new puppy owner might face in achieving that?

I hope this discussion guide is useful. Please feel free to email Beth on hello@packleaderdogadventures.co.uk with your findings, and I'll be sure to reply in due course.

Warmly

Dom Hodgson

About the Author

Dom Hodgson is a dog adventurer, 'superhero' dog trainer and the UK's most respected, sought-after and controversial pet business coach.

In 2011 Dom launched his first business, 'Pack Leader Dog Adventures', which revolutionised the dog walking industry by transforming the usual dog walking services from a 'boring toilet walk around the block' to a training adventure experience that helps busy dog owners with stay-at-home dogs enjoy a full, active and stress-free life.

In 2016 Dom wrote the Amazon-bestselling *How to Be Your Dog's Superhero*, which for the first time delivered a 'real-life' dog training blueprint that any pet dog owner can use to have more control and more fun with their dogs.

The Perfect Puppy Project is the second in the Street-Smart Dog Training manuals, which aim to provide expert help to dog owners suffering from the same common problems. You can pick up other books in the series from Amazon or Audible.

Dom is known as the 'King of Canine Common Sense'. He is an in-demand speaker, and in his dog training seminars and pet business bootcamps he delivers the same unvarnished, no-BS, jargon-free advice he dispenses in his unique writing style, which has won him thousands of dog and human admirers all over the world.

Occasionally, when invited, Dom will travel to speak at dog training clubs and to consult with dog trainers, walkers and groomers to help them grow their business. His seminar attendees describe the experience as hilarious AND life-changing, and his record in helping turn around failing pet businesses is unmatched in the industry.

To enquire about a speaking or pet business consultation email Beth at hello@packleaderdogadventures.co.uk

He lives in an old farmhouse in Sunderland in the North East of England with his wife and best friend, Beth, and two sons, Toby and Alex. Alex is also the Adventure Manager for Pack Leader Dog Adventures.

When not working, Dom can usually be found walking his dogs on the beach or sitting with his hens in the garden.

Other Books by the Author

Dog Training Books

How To Be Your Dog's Superhero: Transform your dastardly dog using the power of play.

Other Books in the Street-Smart Dog Training Series (1–3)

Worry Free Walks – How to transform your difficult, dangerous and devilish dog into a problem-free pooch you are proud to take to the park.

The Perfect Puppy Project– The ultimate no-mess, zero-stress, step-by-step guide to raising the perfect puppy.

The Hungry Games – Discover how you can bin the bowl and use food to play, train and entertain your perfect pet dog.

Pet Business Books

Walk Yourself Wealthy: The quick, easy and no-BS guide to transform your passion for pooches into an insanely profitable and fun dog-walking empire .

Acknowledgements

Huge thanks to the many friends and colleagues who have helped me get my fourth book done in record time.

To my proofreader Nick Jones and publisher, Bill Goss, I say thank you!

To my wonderful illustrator and keeper of the coloured pens, Julia Brown of Brown Owl Design I say Grazi!

To my good friend and small business ass kicker, Vicky Fraser, for all your support and help with this book, I say 'what's next?', and Merci!

To my very good friend and movie maker extraordinaire, Alex 'the video guy' Wardle, I say Kansha!

To my many dog training friends, Pet Business Inner Circle members and my *Diamond* and *Platinum* coaching clients who beta read this for me, I say Danke!

And to my family and friends who are supporting and loving beyond measure I say ta very much. I couldn't do this without you.

And to you, dear reader, for investing in this book and taking time out of your busy day to read it, I say thanks from the bottom of my walking boots. If you got any value from this book at all then please <u>leave a review on Amazon for me.</u> I'm passionate about keeping dogs and their owners together, and the best way for you to help me help more dog owners is to leave a nice review about this book on Amazon or Audible.

To anyone else I've forgotten, I say maybe you should have done more to remind me of your efforts....try harder next time.

Keep it unreal.

Dom

x

Recommended Dog Training Books

The Dog Vinci Code by John Rogerson

Another Pup by Sarah Bartlett

Educating Alice by JJ Fitzpatrick

Pesky Puppy to Perfect Pet by Carol Clark